LE CHOCOLAT

Le Chocolat

MARTINE JOLLY

Translated and adapted by

Philip and Mary Hyman

PANTHEON BOOKS • NEW YORK

*The eighteenth-century silver chocolate pots photographed
on page 9 and facing page 121 were loaned by Monsieur Suger,
Louvre des Antiquaires de Paris.*
Color plates photographed by Daniel Czap.

Library of Congress Cataloging in Publication Data

Jolly, Martine.
Le chocolat.

Translation of: Le chocolat.
1. Cookery (Chocolate)   2. Chocolate.
I. Hyman, Philip.   II. Hyman, Mary.   III. Title.
TX767.CsJ6513 1985   641.6'374   85-3542
ISBN 0-394-54279-7

Book design by Joe Marc Freedman
Manufactured in the United States of America
First American Edition

Contents

CONTENTS

List of Color Plates

I

ALL ABOUT
CHOCOLATE

1

The Origin and History of Chocolate

CHOCOLATE IN THE NEW WORLD

Confronted with legends of the Indians, their oral history, and the amazed accounts of the Spanish conquistadors, it is difficult to know when we are dealing with myth and when with reality. For thousands of years before the discovery of the Americas, Indian civilizations grew, fused together, and disappeared. One of the great Indian civilizations encountered in the sixteenth century hardly existed two hundred years earlier. These people called themselves the *Mexica* or *Azteca of Atzlan* after the mythical place they were believed to have come from. At first, they were no more than a tribe of warriors living near the lagoon of Lake Texcoco at a height of 8,000 feet (2,200 m) above sea level. There, in the course of time, the Aztecs built their capital city, Mexico-Tenochtitlán, and from there extended their empire from the deserted plains in the north to the warm lands in the south, from the Pacific to the Caribbean. Tradition had it that they were descended from the founders of earlier civilizations, in particular from the people of Tula, the Toltecs, who, for the Aztecs, were considered gods.

Quetzalcoatl, the feathered serpent, god of the Toltecs, was the gardener of Paradise, where the first men lived. It was he who taught them how to grow the *cacahuaquahitl*, or cacao tree. The feathered serpent instructed them in the arts, agriculture, and medicine. He was a god of peace and happiness who refused human sacrifices because "he loved his people very much and accepted only snakes, birds, and butterflies in sacrifice." Then one day, Quetzalcoatl was forced out of Paradise by the evil magician Tezcatlipoca. He was last seen, according to legend, floating away on a strange raft made of serpents tied together, heading toward the east and the Red Land of Tlapallán, "from where the sun comes."

Though banished, the good Quetzalcoatl left behind him some successors. One of them, Tlaloc, the god of agriculture and rain, offered his chosen followers a paradise called Tlalocán, a hot and humid land where fruits and cacao trees grew in abundance in luxuriant, rainy orchards.

This sixteenth-century engraving depicts the various stages of the preparation of chocolate by the Indians of New Spain.

He seemed to be a god of peace and happiness. Nevertheless, during the Rain Feasts, in addition to the ceremonial baths in the lagoon, little children were drowned as an offering to Tlaloc.

Tradition has it that it was Hunalpu, the third king of the Mayas, who expanded the cultivation of the cacao tree. Unfortunately, much about the history of that people remains a mystery because the Spanish burned precious documents relating to their past. We do know, however, that they were farmers, and it seems reasonable to assume that they had learned how to grow the cacao tree and to produce cocoa. Existing documents state that the last of the Mayan dynasties received cocoa as a sort of tax from cities they governed and that Mayan traders traveling along the Yucatan coasts used cacao beans as money in their dealings.

With the arrival of the Europeans in the New World, the history of chocolate becomes clearer. What was the situation worldwide at the beginning of the sixteenth century? In 1507, while Montezuma, the second emperor of the Aztecs, was celebrating the Feast of the New Fire—the equivalent in the Aztec calendar of the first day in a new century for us—the Renaissance was sweeping Europe. France was busy fighting wars against both Italy and Spain, while the latter, having triumphed over the Moors and expelled them from Granada, was hungry for new victories and actively started sending fleets across the Atlantic with missionaries and conquistadors to colonize the recently discovered islands in the New World: the Bahamas, Haiti, and Cuba.

During the twenty-seven years that separate Columbus's first voyage to the New World in 1492 and the arrival of Cortés in Mexico, Montezuma II, unaware of what destiny had in store, continued the expansion of his empire to the farthest reaches of the distant tropics. He took control of all the areas then producing cocoa: Tepeaca, Orizaba, Tehuantepec, and Xoconochco (Soconusco), the latter reputedly producing the finest cocoa. He levied taxes that were paid in cocoa beans, which were used not only as currency but also in the preparation of a very important drink. The modern history of cocoa was about to begin.

Indeed, this history might have begun with Columbus and not with Cortés had Columbus taken full advantage of a twist of fate. In 1502, Columbus left Cádiz on his fourth and last trip to the New World. After stopping in Martinique, he continued on into unknown territory and in July 1502 came upon an isle the natives called the Island of Guanaja, and which he renamed the Isle of Pines. His ship was approached by the largest vessel he had yet encountered in the Americas; it was powered by twenty-five strong rowers transporting a richly dressed Indian chief wearing a feathered headdress and embroidered robe. The chief offered Columbus a variety of valuable gifts, but he also seemed interested in trading with the strangers, offering Columbus some brown-colored beans, which he used as money. At the same time, the Indian chief had a drink prepared with some of these beans and offered it to the Europeans to taste. The drink, bitter and spicy, was chocolate, and the first Europeans to taste it found it exceedingly unpleasant. The chief returned to his boat and was rowed away, no doubt with a collection of glass beads, and Columbus set sail again for Europe with the brown beans he had been offered and that he considered unimportant and valueless. Chocolate's time had yet to come in Europe, and several more years would pass before it was finally "discovered."

In 1519, during Holy Week, Cortés and six hundred men dressed in armor and carrying crossbows landed in Mexico on the Tabasco coast. This was the year that Aztec priests had predicted the mythical feathered serpent was to make his return.

Determined to conquer the new land, Cortés burned the boats in which he arrived in order to remove any thoughts of turning back, and prepared to advance. At San Juan de Ulúa, he encountered Pinotl, Aztec governor of the region, and two local dignitaries. What must they have thought of each other, these two representatives of different races and civilizations that had nothing whatsoever in common? Superstition and fear on the part of the Indians and greed on the part of Cortés for the riches the new country seemed to offer apparently prompted both to avoid violence, at least in this early encounter, and to continue the march toward the capital of the Aztecs and the Emperor Montezuma.

When they finally arrived there, Cortés and his faithful companion and chronicler Bernal Díaz del Castillo were stunned by the beauty of Tenochtitlán. They had been told about this city, but little suspected how beautiful it would be, what luxury they would find there, or the well-ordered way in which the city was governed. Cortés wrote back to his king, Charles V, that "the Indians live almost as we do in Spain and in as orderly a fashion," and he went on to describe with astonishment "the logic the Indians seem to apply to all they undertake."

Upon their arrival in Mexico City, Cortés was welcomed by Montezuma in the following terms: "Here you will be given everything you and your men need; consider yourself at home and in your native land." For the Indian ruler, Cortés and his soldiers, coming from the east and being so different from himself and his people, had to be the reincarnation of the good feathered serpent god, Quetzalcoatl. Such an interpretation helped enormously in establishing the Spaniards in their new land, but it would consequently lead to the total annihilation of the young, two-hundred-year-old Indian civilization.

The meeting of the Spanish and the indigenous populations of Mexico paved the way for the introduction of chocolate to Europe.

Four days after Cortés's arrival, Montezuma took him and several of his companions to the top of a great temple—the teocalli—in Tlatelolco. This majestic temple, built in the shape of a pyramid, was the perfect vantage point from which to survey the city and its surroundings: "From the top, we were so high up that we could see everything for miles around." Viewed from above, the city was a model of urban organization: the straight, wide streets were bordered by canals and beautiful buildings with flowering terraces. One could travel from place to place either by foot or by boat. The Spaniards admired the central market and remarked on "the crowds of people assembled to buy and sell merchandise. . . . We all agreed that we had never seen a better-organized market, nor one as big or as packed with people."

Bernal Díaz del Castillo would later visit this same market and admire the diversity of the produce that came from all parts of the empire. There he saw cocoa beans being used both as merchandise and as money. Merchants called *cacahueteros* specialized in the sale of cocoa beans, each labeled with its place of origin: those from Xoconochco (Soconusco) were considered the best. Prices varied depending on where the beans came from and their quality; they could be used to purchase slaves or a chicken for dinner, and they were also used to make a drink the Aztecs called *tchocolatl*. This drink was not to be enjoyed by all—it was drunk only by the emperor, the members of the court, and the army.

The emperor's palace, made of a series of connecting buildings and courtyards, greatly impressed Cortés. He wrote: "This palace is so beautiful that I cannot find words to describe it; all I can say is that it is much grander than anything in Spain." It was in these sumptuous surroundings that the Spanish attended, awestruck, the imperial feasts. Bernal Díaz del Castillo left us a description of one such banquet: "The emperor was seated behind a gilded screen on a low, plush, and richly ornamented chair before a table covered with a white cloth, and he ate, or rather tasted, hundreds of dishes and delectable fruits that were placed in front of him. Everything was served in black or red Cholula pottery. While Montezuma dined, his attendants, who were in an adjoining room, had to be careful not to cause the slightest disturbance. From time to time, a drink made from cocoa was brought to him in a fine, golden chalice; this drink was said to have aphrodisiac virtues. Nearly one hundred fifty pots of good, foamy *tchocolatl* were brought in. It was the drink of Montezuma." When the dinner was finished, the guards and the court could begin their festivities, complete with a show of dancers and singers. In all, they consumed nearly "two thousand pounds of meat and more than two thousand pots of foaming cocoa prepared in the Mexican way."

At the beginning of the Spanish conquest, Cortés paid virtually no attention at all to cocoa. He did not consider using it as currency, and as a drink neither he nor his men liked it. But then Cortés ran short of money, which threatened the continuation of his expedition, and he realized that the cocoa bean could be exchanged for the gold he needed so much. He got Montezuma to give him the royal plantation of Manialtepec and used it as a bank from which he could withdraw as many cocoa beans as he wanted, fix the rate of exchange, and turn them into gold.

Meanwhile, since there was little or no wine on the high Mexican plateaux, the Spanish soldiers became resigned to drinking cocoa, "in order not to have to drink just water all the time," and discovered that "when you drink it, you can travel all day without fatigue, and without having to eat anything else."

It was the custom among the Aztecs to make human sacrifices in order to ensure a good harvest. The planting, the harvesting, and the selection of the cocoa beans were all accompanied by elaborate religious ceremonies. When the cacao pods were ripe, there was a big ceremony in which everyone drank *tchocolatl* while naked warriors decorated with feathers danced, and priests officiated in honor of Tonacatecutli, the goddess of food, and Chalchihuitlicue, the goddess of water.

Carried out within a religious context by women especially designated by Montezuma, the preparation of the Aztecs' chocolate drink was quite complicated. The cocoa beans were first roasted, then ground to a paste and mixed with water. This mixture was heated until the cocoa butter rose to the surface. After being skimmed off, a certain proportion of the cocoa butter was mixed back into the drink, which was vigorously beaten to form a thick foam and drunk cold. Additional ingredients could be added to this basic mixture, such as chili peppers, pepper, vanilla, annatto, or corn flour. The Aztec cocoa drink was therefore spicy and bitter, and one of the Spanish soldiers, Benzo, said "that it would be better thrown to the pigs than consumed by men."

Nevertheless, as the conquerors settled down in the new country, they became accustomed not only to drinking *tchocolatl* but to eating other local foods, such as tomatoes, corn, and turkey, and to smoking tobacco. Unfortunately, relations between the Aztecs and the new occupants began to deteriorate; the latter became more and more demanding toward the natives, whose riches they wanted and whose bloody religious practices they didn't understand, and finally the Aztecs tried to throw the foreign invaders out.

Their failure was absolute. In 1521 everything came to an end when Cortés systematically and totally destroyed Tenochtitlán to make way for the European colonization of Mexico.

Little by little the country found itself peopled by Europeans who had gone there to make their fortunes. The cocoa plantations were developed, but before *tchocolatl* could really take off to become the favorite drink of the Spanish colonists, one more ingredient had to be added: sugar.

Immediately after the discovery of America, the Spanish had taken sugar cane from the Canary Islands and planted it in San Domingo, then in Mexico. It was the idea of mixing sugar, cocoa, and vanilla together that finally made *tchocolatl* pleasant to the European palate, and the nuns in the convent at Oaxaca, whose monastic life did not preclude gastronomic pursuits, invented some delicious recipes, some of which included cinnamon and aniseed.

In Mexico City, public establishments called *chocolaterías* soon opened where people went at the end of the day to relax by listening to native music and sipping foamy chocolate, either hot or cold. From Mexico, chocolate spread throughout Latin America. One Cuban variation, *chocolate de regalo,* included ground corn, and in Venezuela chocolate, or *chorote,* was made with brown sugar.

CHOCOLATE CAPTIVATES SPAIN

T he "chocolate route" began with the return of the Spanish from Mexico to Spain, where they found that they missed what had become their favorite drink. It started in the Gulf of Mexico, the boats driven by "chocolate winds" in the good sailing season. It seems that chocolate began to be known in Spain around 1527, and its use steadily increased over the next twenty-five years.

At first, chocolate was seen as a medicine in Spain, good for curing a variety of ailments and especially recommended for "organic debility," although some people regarded it warily as some sort of magic philter. Finally it was recognized for its nutritious and restorative properties. As recipes for it were refined and simplified to a mixture of cocoa and sugar flavored with cinnamon and vanilla, people found it more and more delicious, until the Spanish developed a real passion for it. Soon noble ladies began to ask their servants to bring them chocolate in church in order to make the long service easier to bear and to strengthen their weakened constitutions. The priests and bishops were furious at this, preaching fire and brimstone and threatening excommunication, which simply prompted the chocolate-besotted ladies to change churches. The real winner in this battle, of course, was chocolate.

As early as 1523, Pietro Martire d'Anghiera was already writing to Pope Clement VII that chocolate was "a fortunate currency," since it did not predispose people to be miserly, and that it had the added advantage of being "a delicious and useful beverage." In the

Cistercian convents, the nuns began to produce chocolate as well as to drink it. At the time, rules concerning religious fasts were extremely strict, and those in religious communities discovered that chocolate helped them through difficult fasting periods by relieving their hunger. The Church was thus confronted with a real problem: was chocolate a food or a drink? As a drink it did not break the fast, but as a food it was strictly forbidden. The canonists haggled over this question for a long time. Finally, in 1662, a cardinal with a penchant for good food, Francesco Maria Brancaccio, handed down his judgment, Solomon-style: "Drinks do not break the fast; wine, though very nourishing, does not break it in the least. The same applies to chocolate, which is undeniably nourishing, but is not, for all that, a food." And as Albert Franklin concludes in his *Private Life in Other Times,* "this was the winning argument for the very good reason that it was in everyone's interest."

An eighteenth-century chocolate pot.

A few years later, in France, Madame de Sévigné, with her Cartesian good sense, kept her good conscience intact by declaring, "I drank some chocolate this morning so that I could fast until evening, and it had just the effect I was looking for. That's why I like it: it allows one to carry out one's good intentions." So in spite of the serious theological question it raised, chocolate was not stopped in its conquest of Europe.

CHOCOLATE CONQUERS EUROPE

For a long time, chocolate was a Spanish specialty and a heavily taxed luxury product. It remained an aristocratic drink within the confines of that country. Then the Spanish introduced chocolate to Flanders, and it began to spread throughout the other European countries.

Around 1606 an Italian named Antonio Carletti, who had lived for many years in the West Indies, showed the Italians how to make chocolate. The drink was an enormous success, and chocolate makers, or *cioccolatieri,* developed hundreds of new ways of preparing it, thus creating a new art. From the cafés of Florence and Venice, news of their talent spread, and people sent for Italian chocolate makers from all over Europe.

Chocolate entered France through the front door. On October 25, 1615, the young king of France, Louis XIII, married a Spanish princess, Anne of Austria, daughter of King Philip III. She loved chocolate and had brought everything necessary for preparing it with her. To get into the good graces of the new queen, the members of the court began drinking her favorite beverage and developed a tremendous taste for it. Richelieu's brother, the cardinal of Lyons, was a real fan. He drank it often "to temper the vapors of

It was under the reign of Louis XIV that chocolate became fashionable at court and in literary salons.

the spleen and fight against biliousness and bad humor." At midcentury Philip of Orleans became so infatuated with chocolate that he drank it every morning for breakfast and invited the court to this ceremony: upon rising in the morning, he left his bedroom and went to drink his chocolate in a large room, where the courtiers could come to greet him. They had "gained admission to chocolate."

It was probably about 1646 that Johan Georg Volckammer, a Nuremberg scholar, brought chocolate back from Naples, where he had been visiting. At first, the Germans were hesitant to taste it, but when they did, it became a veritable passion, and something to which they attributed aphrodisiac qualities. It was said that in good bourgeois households in Germany, a nightly cup of chocolate was *de rigueur*. But the German government levied a heavy tax on the drink, and thereafter only the very rich could afford it.

A few years later, in 1657, chocolate arrived in England. At first considered an extravagance limited to only the highest social circles, it nevertheless caught on relatively quickly. People began serving it in cafés and clubs, and in 1674, a famous London café, At the Coffee Mill and Tobacco Roll, began serving chocolate cakes and "Spanish style" confections. In 1746 the famous Cacaotree chocolate club was founded whose members invented new chocolate preparations. Among their innovations was the replacement of water by milk and the addition of various other ingredients, such as eggs, alcohols, old wine, port, or Madeira.

CHOCOLATE IN THE UNITED STATES

While the English were discovering the delights of chocolate, their American colonies were being extended along the Atlantic coast. Strong commercial ties linked these colonies to England, who sent them sugar, tea, and chocolate, among other products. Chocolate arrived in colonial America, not as cocoa beans to be processed, but as large bars of chocolate ready for use.

The Americans were not to be totally dependent on the British for long. Around 1760, a group of fishermen in Gloucester, Massachusetts, accepted cocoa beans in exchange for fish they furnished to a newly arrived ship from the West Indies. This was the first time that cocoa beans had entered the country. Several years later, the first American chocolate factory was established in Dorchester, Massachusetts, by an English manufacturer, John Hannon, and James Baker, a financier. Baker's Chocolate, which exists to this day, is therefore the oldest American chocolate.

The American love of chocolate grew at a rapid pace from that moment on—much faster than on the other side of the Atlantic. Beans were imported directly from the West Indies, and more and more chocolate factories sprang up throughout the nineteenth century. By 1897, the United States was importing 77,390 tons of cocoa beans from Ecuador, Trinidad, Brazil, and Angola.

Today, American chocolate lovers have their own newsletter, published every other month by Milton Zelman and called *Chocolate News*. It keeps them informed of the latest chocolate "developments" in the United States and elsewhere, and has been a great success. (For subscription information, write *Chocolate News*, 40 West 20th Street, Suite 901-A, New York, New York 10011.) Several times a year, chocolate fanatics meet in cities across the country for Chocolate Lovers' Weekends, where "chocoholics" raise their voices in song ("I'm a chocoholic and I'm proud . . .") and eat chocolate preparations during the entire affair.

From those early days, when colonial housewives made chocolate confections in their kitchens, up until the present, when chocolate has become a major industry, a long and glorious path has been traveled by generations of American chocolate lovers. Today it is estimated that Americans consume approximately 1.8 billion pounds of chocolate a year, costing 3 billion dollars annually.

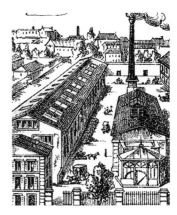

The Industrial Revolution transformed the production of chocolate, making it available to the general public.

THE FABRICATION OF CHOCOLATE

F|or most of the eighteenth century, the fabrication of chocolate was an artisanal trade, with every step of its preparation, from the cocoa bean to the finished product, done by hand. Then in 1777, a man in Barcelona by the name of Fernández, who took the title of "chocolate maker of Madame la Dauphine and of the princes and lords of the court," manufactured chocolate with the aid of machines for the first time in history. The artisanal period, which had lasted from the beginning of the sixteenth century to the end of the eighteenth, had ended. The French Revolution and other political upheavals slowed the industrialization of chocolate manufacture momentarily, but it picked up speed with the turn of the century. At the same time, the cultivation of the cacao tree and the mechanization of chocolate making were being developed in more and more countries throughout the world.

In 1819, François Louis Cailler, a Swiss who had gone to learn the art of chocolate making in Turin, came back to his native country and set up the first real chocolate factory, in a cocoa mill just outside of Vevey, Switzerland. At just the same time, the count of Lasteyrie was putting the finishing touches on a new triple mill he had just developed. In Amsterdam, the mills of Van Houten and

Booker had been turning since 1815, and in 1824, at Noisiel-sur-Marne in France, Antoine Brutus Menier founded the first chocolate factory built on a large enough scale to respond to a worldwide demand.

But the search for new recipes continued, especially in Switzerland, and finally, in 1875, Daniel Peter discovered how to make milk chocolate. With the help of Henri Nestlé, who had just developed a new method for making condensed milk, the process for making milk chocolate was improved and refined until, in 1905, the Peter factory began to produce it, using a Nestlé company recipe.

Some years after Nestlé and Peter first began making milk chocolate with condensed milk, Milton Hershey devised a way of using whole milk to make milk chocolate and, in 1893, gave Americans their first taste of the Hershey bar they like so much today. In 1895, the Hershey company perfected its product by adding almonds to it, opening the door to an almost endless number of mixtures, far removed from the original dark chocolate bar made simply from chocolate liquor and sugar.

The wonderful, magical story of chocolate, born in legend, with all the ups and downs of a difficult but glorious conquest of Europe and America, had come to an end. Today the product of a highly developed international industry, chocolate is eaten with pleasure by people all over the world, a far cry from the bitter drink of Quetzalcoatl.

2

Some Notes on the Botany and Harvesting of Chocolate

BOTANY

otanically, the cacao tree is known under the scientific name of *Theobroma cacao, L.* *Theobroma* is a Greek word meaning "drink of the gods." *Cacao* is the Spanish rendition of the Aztec *cacahuatl. L.* stands for Linnaeus, the Swedish botanist who classified it under the name *Theobroma cacao*.

There are three varieties of *Theobroma cacao, L.*:

The *criollo:* This is the original cacao tree, the one the Spanish found when they discovered Mexico. It is still cultivated in South America, in Colombia and Venezuela, but is no longer planted in Mexico, its country of origin. The pod is elongated, with small, round, pale-colored beans containing very little tannin. This variety is used exclusively in the making of very fine chocolates. Unfortunately, it is not hardy and has a very low yield.

The *forastero:* This word means "foreign," and the variety originally came from the upper Amazon region. The pods are rounded, containing flat beans that furnish the cocoa highest in tannin content. This variety of cacao is the most widely cultivated and includes the African trees with a very high yield.

The *trinitario:* Apparently a cross between the first two varieties, this one combines characteristics of both. The quality of the cocoa it furnishes is much closer to that of the *forastero*.

The leaves, flowers, and fruits of the cacao tree. On the right is pictured an open cacao pod with the beans inside.

One could naively think that this "gift of the gods" grows like a weed and offers up its goodness for the asking, demanding only that one take the time to pick the fruits, as in some earthly paradise. This is far from the case, and in fact, the chocolate we are so fond of is, in the end, the result of pure chance as far as its reproduction is concerned, and dependent on human imagination for its manufacture.

First of all, the cacao tree will grow only at an altitude of about 2,000 feet (600 m) and only within the magical band that encircles the globe between the twenty-first and twenty-second parallels, between Réunion Island and Cuba, for instance, as southern and northern limits. It is within this same band that products such as coffee, sugar cane, and vanilla flourish. The cacao tree likes heat and moisture, but not excessively hot sun, so it is happiest in the shadow of the great tropical forests. This means that anyone who wants to start a cacao plantation first has to plant large trees that can shade the 13- to 20-foot (4 to 6 m) cacao trees.

This unusual tree has leaves, fruits, and flowers all at the same time; although there are several growths of leaves in the course of a year, the tree is constantly in flower. This does not mean, however, that it is particularly fertile. The small pink or white flowers have no smell, and they grow directly on the trunk or large branches of the tree. They last only forty-eight hours, and although they are both male and female, they depend on a certain gnat to pollinize them with the thick pollen—since they have no smell, other pollen carriers are not attracted to them. Although a single tree can have up to 50,000 to 100,000 flowers in a twelve-month period, because of the difficulty of pollinization only about 1 flower in 500 bears fruit—but what a fruit!

Called a cacao pod, the fruit of the cacao tree is roughly the shape of a quince. It can be anywhere from 6 to 12 inches (15 to 30 cm) long, and 3 to 4 inches (7 to 10 cm) wide and grows, like the flower from which it issues, directly on the trunk or branches of the tree. The color of the pod depends on the variety, and it changes as it ripens: a young green fruit ripens to yellow, a reddish-purple one turns orange. The pod is very hard, with about forty cocoa beans inside, nestled in a sweet pulp that diminishes as the fruit ripens. Like an ordinary bean, the cocoa bean is made up of two halves, with a "germ" or sprout in the middle enclosed within a tannin-rich envelope. It's difficult to imagine that these bitter, acrid beans contain what we know as cocoa and it is only after an elaborate treatment that they will be turned into chocolate. On average, about twenty pods yield about 2¼ pounds (1 kg) of dried beans—and an annual yield of 1,000 to 1,500 pounds per acre (1 to 1.5 metric tons per hectare) is considered excellent.

The cacao tree lives for about forty years, during which time it must be cared for regularly to ensure sufficient shade to protect it from the tropical sun, as well as to prevent the attack of various insects, parasites, and diseases.

HARVESTING

I n countries with a steady rainfall and no real dry season, cacao pods can be harvested all year round, but in places with marked rainy and dry seasons, there are two harvests a year.

The pod is ripe about four to six months after fertilization of the flower. The ripeness of the fruit is judged not only according to color (yellow or orange, according to the type) but also by the noise it makes when tapped or knocked. When it makes a dull thump, and the beans can be heard rattling against each other, the pod is ready to be harvested.

To pick a pod takes know-how and dexterity, because the stem must be cut with a very sharp knife without damaging the dormant flower buds just behind it, which could develop in turn into new flowers and fruits themselves. Next, the pods have to be split in half lengthwise in order to remove the beans. One must be careful to split the pod with a single blow, without damaging the beans inside. This demands enormous manpower because it is done by hand, although mechanical shelling machines are now beginning to be used.

Once the beans have been extracted from the pods, they are subjected to a period of fermentation, destined to remove the sticky pulp and make the bean swell. There are two ways of doing this: on small plantations, large racks are covered with a bed of leaves that are pierced with holes to allow the liquid that exudes from the cocoa beans to run off. The beans are spread out, then covered. In a large plantation, the beans are placed in special vats made of wood or cement that have an opening at the top and a drain for the liquid at the bottom.

During this period of fermentation, the bitterness and astringency of the beans is reduced, and what the planters call the forerunners of the aroma begin to appear. How much the beans have swollen, their smell, and the development of a rich brown color are the signs that determine when the fermentation should be stopped. At this point the cocoa bean is beginning to smell like cocoa, and it is finally possible to imagine that it could be made into a substance called chocolate.

To stop the fermentation, the beans are spread out on large cement surfaces to dry in the sun for about two weeks. They are mixed and stirred at regular intervals to ensure even drying. In

Some dark brown cocoa beans before their transformation into chocolate.

certain parts of Central and South America, the workers still do the "cacao dance," which consists of dragging their feet through the beans to a rhythmical chant. This mixing and drying rids the beans of any dull or scaly particles and gives them a characteristic sheen.

Here ends the saga of the cocoa bean in its home countries. The last changes in its transformation into chocolate will come after the beans are poured into sacks, loaded onto ships, and transported over the wide oceans to faraway places.

3

The Manufacture of Chocolate

A fter their long voyage, the cocoa beans arrive at the chocolate factory. What happens now? As one might imagine, the answer isn't simple.

Quality Control

First the beans are subjected to a very strict quality control. The shipment must not present any strange smell or taste, contain any foreign matter or more than a certain percentage of defective beans, and the beans' water content must be within acceptable limits.

Cleaning

Because the beans are necessarily mixed with dust and other small particles, they then pass over a moving screen that sifts out any impurities.

Roasting

Like coffee, cocoa does not develop its characteristic taste, aroma, and rich brown color until the beans have been roasted. This is a delicate operation because the roast depends not only upon the quality of the beans but also on the roasting process itself. Basically, the higher the quality, the lighter the roast.

Roasting used to take place in rotating spheres for a specific time at a specific temperature; this is still pretty much the case today, except that large rotating drums are used instead of spheres. The cocoa beans are roasted slowly for anywhere from 25 to 50 minutes, at temperatures ranging from 230° to 300°F (110° to 150°C), depending on the quality. As the end of the time approaches, the flair of the specialist comes into play, for he must determine the precise moment at which the beans have reached the perfect development of their aroma and taste, when all of their moisture has evaporated but before they begin to burn. At that moment, the roasting process is immediately stopped and the beans cooled by ventilation.

Top: *The cocoa beans, cleaned of any impurities, are slowly roasted in large, rotating spheres.*
Bottom: *After being roasted, the beans are conveyed to the crushing and winnowing machines, then on to a separating cylinder.*

Crushing

Once the beans have been cooled, they are conveyed to a crushing and winnowing machine to separate them from the germ and the shells, which have become hard and brittle during the roasting process. The beans leave this machine in irregular pieces called cocoa nibs.

Milling

The nibs now pass through a battery of mills. Under the effect of the high temperature and pressure to which the grinding process subjects them, the cocoa butter, which makes up 50 to 60 percent of the cell tissues, is released. The nibs, which were solid and dry, now form a semiliquid mass, a suspension of cocoa particles in the cocoa butter. This chocolate liquor will now undergo one of two treatments, depending upon whether it is to be transformed into cocoa powder or chocolate.

Cocoa Powder

Cocoa powder is a fine powder with a low percentage of cocoa butter (8 to 24 percent). There are three to four steps to the process of converting the chocolate liquor to cocoa powder, depending on the method used.

If the Dutch processing method is used, the chocolate liquor is first treated with an alkali to reduce acidity, enhance flavor, and increase solubility (this was the technique used by the Aztecs).

Whether or not it has been treated with an alkali, the chocolate liquor is then ground extremely fine by passing through a battery of millstones or steel roll refiners.

Next the chocolate liquor is homogenized and heated to a temperature of about 212°F (100°C) and pressed through hydraulic filter presses to squeeze out a specific amount of the cocoa butter (76 to 92 percent). This cocoa butter is filtered and poured into molds—it is a valuable product that will be used in the making of chocolate. The cocoa, on the other hand, is now in the form of a solid mass called a presscake.

The presscake is cooled, crushed, ground, and sifted. The fine powder that is obtained is subjected to an air-conditioned ventilation to ensure its light texture and rich color.

Cocoa powder is classified according to its fat content:

1. Unsweetened cocoa powders
   Only unsweetened cocoa powder should be used in cooking. There are three grades according to U.S. government standards:

LE CHOCOLAT

- *Breakfast cocoa* must contain at least 22 percent fat content.
- *Cocoa* must contain from 10 to 22 percent fat.
- *Low-fat cocoa* must contain less than 10 percent fat.

2. Sweetened cocoa powders
   These are used for making hot cocoa, but should not be used for cooking (unless specifically called for). There are two basic types:
   - *Instant cocoa* is cocoa plus sugar.
   - *Hot cocoa mix* is cocoa plus sugar plus powdered milk.

Cocoa powder has fed the imagination of millions of children.

Chocolate

The chocolate liquor may also be turned into chocolate rather than cocoa powder. In this case, the cocoa butter is not extracted but left in, and any variety of ingredients (sugar, cocoa butter, milk, spices, nuts, and so on) may be added, depending upon what type of chocolate is desired. The amount of sugar determines how sweet or bitter the chocolate will be; the cocoa butter makes it snap cleanly when broken and imparts a certain creaminess; milk makes it softer, sweeter, and more nutritious.

Once the composition of the finished chocolate has been decided upon, it is kneaded in a *mélangeur*, or paste mixer, until perfectly homogenous. At this point it tastes good, but is still grainy, so it is passed through a series of steel roll refiners with smaller and smaller openings and at higher and higher speeds until it comes out in a thin, hard sheet.

You may think that we now have chocolate. No, not yet! It is during the next stage, the conching process, that the chocolate will attain its creamy texture. Many people consider this to be the most important step in chocolate manufacture, and one of my friends, a manufacturer of handmade chocolate, will allow no one but himself to accomplish the conching of his chocolate in order to be sure that it is exactly the way he wants it.

Conching

This process is in fact an additional kneading done in a special kneading trough that was originally in the shape of a shell and called a *concha* (for shell) in Spanish. Cocoa butter is added to the chocolate that comes from the roll refiners and kneaded slowly at a specific temperature that varies depending upon the texture and quality of the finished product. The conching process is a long, slow one, which can last from several hours to several days. It is during conching that the final flavorings are added.

To make semisweet chocolate, the cocoa liquor is mixed with sugar and then mixed and crushed in a series of machines until homogeneous and smooth.

Tempering

Throughout all of the processes that the chocolate liquor goes through on its way to becoming chocolate, it is kept at a relatively high temperature so that the cocoa butter will not solidify. Now it is necessary to cool it down in such a way that the cocoa butter will not separate out and form a whitish film on the finished chocolate. In other words, it must be stabilized. This is done by cooling the chocolate down, while being agitated, to a temperature below the melting point of the cocoa butter crystals, then reheating it just enough to melt unstable types of crystals without melting the stable ones (about 82° to 84°F [28° to 29°C] for milk chocolate, 84° to 86°F [29° to 30°C] for dark chocolate).

Molding

Once the chocolate has been tempered, it is ready to be poured into molds and sent out into the world to satisfy our needs and desires.

The Types of Chocolate

1. COOKING CHOCOLATE

Basically, any chocolate labeled unsweetened (or bitter, or pure), extra bittersweet, bittersweet, or semisweet may be used in cooking, and the higher the quality, the better your dessert or candy will be.

In this book, most recipes call for semisweet or bittersweet chocolate. Before going any further, it is necessary to discuss American labeling for chocolate, according to U.S. government standards:

- *Unsweetened (bitter, pure) chocolate* is 100 percent chocolate liquor (no sugar or flavoring added).
- *Semisweet, bittersweet, and extra bittersweet* must contain a minimum of 35 percent chocolate liquor, but can contain anywhere from 35 to 60 percent. Although the chocolate-liquor content is not necessarily indicated on the package, try to use high-quality chocolate with at least 50 percent. In this book, when the term *bittersweet* is used, try to use a chocolate with at least 55 percent chocolate liquor if possible. In general, Baker's semisweet chocolate gives fine results, but if you are a real chocolate lover, use the chocolate that tastes best to you: the taste of the chocolate you use will come through in the finished dessert. Some of my own favorites are Hershey's Special Dark Chocolate, Cadbury Dark Chocolate, Lindt Excellence, Lindt Extra-Bittersweet, Suchard Bittra, Van Houten, Droste Semisweet, and Tobler Extra-Bittersweet.

2. MILK CHOCOLATE

Milk chocolate must contain a minimum of 10 percent chocolate liquor and 12 percent milk solids. It should not be used in cooking unless specifically called for.

3. OTHER TYPES OF CHOCOLATE

- *Sweet chocolate* must contain at least 15 percent chocolate liquor. Do not use it in cooking, however, because it will not give enough of a chocolate taste.
- *Coating chocolate (couverture)* is basically a semisweet chocolate with added cocoa butter to give a very high gloss to dipped chocolate candies. It is used most often by professional chocolate makers, but can be found in some specialty shops.
- *White chocolate* is not chocolate in the true sense of the term, since it does not contain any cocoa. High-quality white chocolate is made with cocoa butter, sugar, vegetable oils, milk, and vanilla, but lower grades do not use any cocoa butter at all. Good white chocolate has a very creamy texture and subtle flavor not unlike that of butterscotch.

The finished chocolate is weighed, then tempered and poured into the molds that will give it its finished form.

4

The Virtues of Chocolate

Chocolate is unlike any other food, and people have never been indifferent to it. It has been the source of impassioned discussions and reams of literature.

At the very beginning of the story of chocolate, Bernal Díaz del Castillo, the historian of the Spanish conquest of Mexico, wrote: "When one has drunk of this beverage, one can travel all day without fatigue and without taking any other nourishment." When the drink arrived in Spain, its tonic properties were quickly recognized, and it was prescribed as a medicine for the weak and rickety. Antonio Comanero wrote an entire treatise called *Naturaleza y Calidad del Chocolate*, which contained complicated recipes for chocolate, each one adapted for the treatment of a specific ailment. Then it was decided that chocolate was particularly suited to scholars, therefore to theologians and priests, who latched onto it as a pleasant way to make the long Lenten fasts more bearable. So, too, the noble ladies who piously attended the long church services found that a cup of chocolate broke the monotony and gave them newfound strength. In spite of themselves, seventeenth-century Spaniards would accept virtually any excuse for stuffing themselves with chocolate.

In France, although it started out as the drink of the queen and gained favor after that, it was also considered especially for its curative properties. In 1684, a student by the name of Foucault wrote his dissertation on the virtues of chocolate in enthusiastic terms. At the same period, Théophile Dufour declared that it rendered great service to people with "weakened stomachs," and that it was so nourishing "that there is not a meat bouillon that strengthens so much, nor for as long a time. Many people who were obliged to take bouillon several times a day for their health found that they could drink three cups of chocolate a day, with no other nourishment for several days, and suffer no ill effects whatsoever." A certain Doctor Blégny praised the merits of the chocolate he prepared, "so that those who like chocolate and had the misfortune of being afflicted by that most universal of gallant maladies"—presumably lovesickness—"shall know that they can find in it the enlightenment necessary to console them."

From the Aztecs to the breakfast chocolate of children, chocolate has come a long way.

For Doctor Hecquet, a medical school dean in the early eighteenth century, chocolate was not a drink, but rather a bouillon or consommé "so nourishing as to be able to strengthen the most robust people," and Nicolas Audry, one of his colleagues, affirmed that it would cure pulmonary consumption. In 1705 in Holland, Doctor Stephani Blancardi gave forth a veritable concerto of praises for chocolate as a drink that is not only pleasurable but that has other advantages as well: "Chocolate is not only delicious in taste, but it is also an absolute balm for the mouth, keeping the mucous membranes and glands in good health. This is why those who drink it have such sweet breath."

Finally, in the nineteenth century, in *The Physiology of Taste*, Brillat-Savarin wrote at length about chocolate: "Chocolate is as healthy a drink as it is pleasant . . . it is to be recommended for people given to intense mental concentration . . . indeed it suits the weakest stomachs." And: "Every man who feels temporarily that he has become foolish; every man who finds the hours long and the atmosphere difficult to stand; every man who becomes obsessed with an idea that takes away his freedom to think: every one of them, I say, should take a good pint dose of chocolate flavored with ambergris."

Today, you will find no chocolate flavored with ambergris (one of Brillat-Savarin's recipes), but I know of some forms of chocolate that I guarantee will have the same effect.

Many of them are in this book!

II

THE RECIPES

SOME PRELIMINARY ADVICE

Baking demands that you be even more organized than you are for cooking; one simply can't improvise at the last minute. Baking is a precise and demanding art.

Before beginning anything, make sure that you have all the ingredients you need at hand; if not, make a shopping list before setting out to get them.

Figure out how much time you can devote to your dessert. Desserts hate to be hurried, so choose them according to your time and the kind of meal you plan to serve: some may be made in advance, others have to be made at the last minute. This is indicated at the beginning of each recipe.

Before beginning the recipe itself, carefully read the list of ingredients. Measure them and set them out on the table, as well as all the utensils you will need.

If using the oven, preheat it to the temperature indicated before you do anything else, even if it takes longer to prepare the dough or batter than it does for the oven to heat up.

Although precise preparation times are given for all of the recipes, don't follow them blindly. They are there simply to give you a rough idea of how much time you will need. Obviously, an experienced cook will work much faster than an inexperienced one, and no two pans, stoves, or ovens are the same. As much as possible, "signs of doneness" are indicated in the recipe to guide you.

Follow the measurements scrupulously. Of course, you can halve or double them, but the relative proportions of the ingredients must be respected. Only the seasonings escape this rule, since a little more or a little less cinnamon, vanilla, or alcohol won't change the appearance or texture of the basic mixture.

Know your oven. The thermostat markings or temperatures indicated on it are approximate; no two ovens are alike. Since it is essential that cakes, cookies, and pastries be cooked correctly, only time and experience will tell you whether you can rely on the temperatures and cooking times indicated in a recipe, or whether you have to set your oven slightly hotter or cooler, or bake for a longer or shorter time than it says.

Never make a dessert you haven't made before when you have invited people to dinner. Test the recipe first with your family or very close friends who don't mind a disaster! This applies to cooking in general: how many unpleasant surprises could be avoided if only this rule were followed!

Have the correct utensils on hand; they make everything so much easier.

UTENSILS NEEDED FOR THE RECIPES IN THIS BOOK

- A set of 5 saucepans ranging from about 5 to 8½ inches (13 to 22 cm) in diameter
- A set of 3 frying pans (preferably nonstick) measuring approximately 6, 8, and 9½ inches (15, 20, and 24 cm) in diameter respectively
- 2 blini pans (optional)
- 3 soufflé molds measuring about 5½, 7, and 8½ inches (14, 18, and 22 cm) in diameter respectively
- 2 charlotte molds, about 5½ and 6¼ inches (14 and 16 cm) in diameter respectively, or 1- and 1½-quart (1 and 1½ l) capacities
- A round cake pan 8½ inches (22 cm) in diameter
- A rectangular cake pan 8 by 12 inches (20 by 30 cm)
- An 8-inch (20 cm) loaf pan, about 1-quart (1 l) capacity
- 12 to 16 petit-four tartlet molds, 1¼ to 1½ inches in diameter
- 8 to 12 nonstick tartlet molds, 2¾ to 3½ inches (7 to 9 cm) in diameter
- Ramekin molds
- A set of mixing bowls

- A set of smaller bowls
- Plastic boxes for storage

For mixing, etc.

- A food processor for pureeing, grating, chopping, and mixing (optional)
- An electric mixer
- A scale (if possible) and measuring cups
- 2 sieves, large and small
- A set of good kitchen knives, including one serrated knife
- 2 to 3 wooden spoons
- 2 wooden spatulas
- A long, flexible-blade metal spatula
- A plastic or rubber scraper
- A skimmer or slotted spoon
- 2 ladles, medium and small
- 2 wire whisks, large and small
- 2 cake racks, one round, one rectangular
- A pastry board
- A rolling pin
- A marble slab (or heavy baking sheet)
- 2 pastry bags, with a complete set of nozzles
- An ice-cream freezer
- A candy thermometer

SOME TIPS ON COOKING WITH CHOCOLATE

Choosing Chocolate

There are many types of chocolate (see discussion on pages 20–21), not to mention chocolate candies of all kinds. To satisfy one's chocolate craving means different things to different people: children often prefer milk chocolate, whereas adults often prefer dark chocolate, ranging from semisweet to bittersweet in taste.

Since the percentage of chocolate liquor in a particular chocolate is not always indicated in the United States, taste is often the only guide: choose a dark chocolate that has a good but slightly bitter taste to you. Baker's semisweet chocolate works very well in all of these recipes, but you may prefer to use a high-quality eating chocolate instead. The better the chocolate, the better the end result.

Melting Chocolate

IN A SAUCEPAN, WITH WATER

This is the method most often used in this book. Break the chocolate into individual squares or pieces. Place in a saucepan with the water (or other liquid) indicated—count about 2 teaspoons liquid for every ounce (30 g) of chocolate called for. Use a saucepan large enough so that all, or nearly all, of the pieces of chocolate can sit on the bottom. Place over very low heat to melt, tapping the chocolate down into the water with a wooden spoon from time to time. When all the pieces of chocolate seem completely soft, stir to make a smooth, creamy mixture. (If the chocolate becomes more and more grainy as you stir, add a little more water. If it is still grainy, it is either of dubious quality or has gotten too hot, and you will simply have to start over again. Melted chocolate should feel warm, not hot, to the touch.) Proceed with the recipe as described.

IN A DOUBLE BOILER

Either a real double boiler or a glass or metal mixing bowl set over a saucepan of simmering water may be used. The water should *not* touch the bottom of the receptacle the chocolate is in, and it should just simmer, not boil. If you cover the double boiler or bowl, the chocolate will melt faster. When all the pieces of chocolate seem soft, stir until smooth.

This method is used only occasionally in this book. Check the chocolate to make sure that it feels only warm—if it begins to feel hot, remove from above the water immediately. Do not allow even one drop of water to fall into the chocolate if melted in this manner, or it will immediately become grainy when stirred.

A FEW THINGS YOU MUST REMEMBER WHEN MAKING THESE RECIPES

- *Butter* always means unsalted butter.
- *Eggs* should be medium eggs (1¾ ounces each or 21 ounces per dozen).
- *Flour* should always be measured as it comes from the package. If you wish to sift it, do so after measuring. Either all-purpose or cake flour may be used.
- *Measurements* are given in the American cup-and-tablespoon system followed by the corresponding metric measurement in parentheses. Since the American-metric equivalents are not exact but approximate, use only one system when doing a given recipe, that is, either American or metric, not a combination of both. Since metric measurements of less than 3 tablespoons (50 ml) do not appear on standard measuring cups, either in France or the United States, amounts less than this are expressed only in tablespoons or teaspoons.
- *Crème fraîche* may be bought in many specialty shops and used in the recipes that call for it, if desired. However, heavy cream may always be substituted for it, as indicated in the recipes in question.

   Crème fraîche may also be made at home: Heat 1 cup (¼ l) pasteurized (*not* ultra-pasteurized) heavy cream to lukewarm. Remove from the heat, stir in 2 tablespoons buttermilk, cover, and allow to sit for 6 to 10 hours in a warm place. When a thick layer has formed on top of the cream, stir well, pour into a jar, cover tightly, and refrigerate overnight before using to allow the cream to thicken uniformly. *Crème fraîche* will keep for about 1 week in the refrigerator.

1

Mousses
Custards and Creams
Frozen Desserts

T hese easy-to-make desserts are extremely versatile. The mousses and pastry creams, for example, can be eaten alone or used as fillings for cakes. In the unlikely event you have any left over, they can be used as a garnish for other desserts or as part of a combination dessert.

But whether you eat them as they are, accompanied perhaps by some crisp cookies to add a crunchy note, or in combination with something else, they all tickle the palate of the chocolate lover.

Chocolate Mousse

MOUSSE AU CHOCOLAT

INGREDIENTS FOR 6 TO 8 SERVINGS

14 ounces (400 g) bittersweet chocolate
6 tablespoons (90 ml) water
6½ tablespoons (100 g) butter, cut into 7 pieces and allowed to soften
5 egg yolks
6 egg whites
1 pinch salt

T his "classic" mousse has a relatively firm texture; it's best to make it a day ahead of time.

Procedure

Place the chocolate and water in a small saucepan and melt as described on page 29. When smooth and creamy, remove from the heat and stir in the butter, piece by piece.

One by one, stir in the egg yolks.

Place the egg whites in a large mixing bowl with the salt. Beat until very stiff. Pour the chocolate over the egg whites and fold it in carefully. The finished mixture should be of uniform color and texture.

Pour the mousse into a serving dish and place in the refrigerator to set. Serve with crisp cookies.

Variations

1. With Coffee: Replace the water with strong coffee and make exactly as described.

2. With Cinnamon: Add 1 teaspoon ground cinnamon to the chocolate and water in the beginning and make exactly as described.

3. With Candied Orange Peel: Soak 1¾ ounces (50 g) candied orange peel in warm water for 1 hour to soften. Drain, pat dry, and dice into very small pieces (you should have about ¼ cup diced orange peel). After folding the egg whites into the mousse, fold in the orange peel along with 1 tablespoon Grand Marnier liqueur, making sure the orange peel is evenly distributed. Chill and serve as described.

4. With Grilled Almonds: Brown 1⅔ cups (135 g) slivered almonds under the broiler as described on page 118. Set aside ⅓ of them, and grind the others to a powder in a heavy-duty blender or food processor. When making the mousse, melt the chocolate in 6 tablespoons (90 ml) strong coffee instead of water. Continue as described. After folding in the egg whites, fold in the ground almonds. Transfer to a serving bowl or individual serving dishes, sprinkle with the reserved almonds, and place in the refrigerator to set before serving.

Whipped-Cream Chocolate Mousse

MOUSSE À LA CRÈME FOUETTÉE

A light, creamy chocolate mousse, this dessert should be made at least several hours to a day in advance.

Procedure

Place the chocolate and water in a small saucepan and melt as described on page 29. When perfectly smooth and creamy, remove from the heat and stir in the egg yolks, one at a time. Allow to cool.

Place the cream and vanilla sugar in a chilled mixing bowl (both the cream and the bowl should be very cold). Beat the cream until it forms soft peaks. Pour the chocolate onto the whipped cream and carefully fold it in.

Place the egg whites and salt in a large mixing bowl and beat until stiff. Fold the chocolate-cream mixture into the whites; the finished mixture should be of uniform color and texture.

INGREDIENTS FOR 6 SERVINGS

9 ounces (250 g) bittersweet chocolate
¼ cup (60 ml) water
4 egg yolks
Generous ¾ cup (200 ml) heavy (whipping) cream, chilled
2 teaspoons vanilla sugar (see note to Whipped Cream with Melted Chocolate, p. 125)
2 egg whites
1 pinch salt

Pour the mousse into a serving bowl and place in the refrigerator to set (if preferred, the mousse may be divided up among individual serving dishes).

Vanilla wafers or other thin, crisp cookies are an excellent accompaniment to this dessert.

Variations

Although this mousse is delicious as is, it may be flavored with various alcohols or liqueurs: whiskey, Grand Marnier, crème de cacao, and so on. Fold the chosen flavor into the mousse just before placing it in the serving dish to chill. Flavor it to suit your taste (generally about 1 tablespoon alcohol is sufficient).

White Chocolate Mousse with Raisins

MOUSSE BLANCHE LÉGÈRE AUX RAISINS

INGREDIENTS FOR 4 TO 6 SERVINGS

¼ cup (50 g) golden raisins
3 tablespoons (50 ml) light rum
1 tablespoon water (for the raisins)
5½ ounces (160 g) white chocolate, broken into pieces
2 tablespoons water (for the white chocolate)
5 tablespoons (75 g) butter, cut into 5 pieces and allowed to soften
4 egg yolks
4 egg whites
1 pinch salt
Hot Chocolate Sauce (p. 120)

PREPARATION TIME

20 to 25 minutes, plus several hours to set

T he sweet, delicate flavor of white chocolate and raisins is contrasted here with the rich taste of the dark chocolate sauce. It is a dessert that should be made a day ahead of time.

Procedure

Place the raisins, rum, and water in a small bowl and allow to sit for 30 minutes.

Meanwhile, melt the white chocolate with the water in a small saucepan over low heat. Swirl the saucepan a couple of times to help the chocolate melt more evenly. When completely melted, stir to make it smooth and creamy, then, away from the heat, stir in the butter, piece by piece.

One by one, stir in the egg yolks. Allow to cool completely.

Place the egg whites and salt in a large mixing bowl and beat until stiff. Pour the white chocolate mixture onto the whites and fold it in carefully; the finished mixture should be of uniform color and texture.

Drain the raisins and pat them dry in a clean cloth or dish towel. Carefully fold them into the mousse, then transfer the mousse to a serving dish and place it in the refrigerator until the next day.

Just before serving, make the Hot Chocolate Sauce; serve the mousse in the serving dish and the sauce in a sauceboat. Or, if you prefer, the mousse may be spooned onto individual dessert plates in a dome and the chocolate sauce poured around it.

Homemade vanilla wafers or other thin, crisp cookies make a nice accompaniment to this dessert.

Chocolate Marquise with Coffee Sauce

MARQUISE AU CAFÉ

Although this is more like a very dense, chilled, chocolate cake than a mousse, I have included the marquise here, since it is made the way a mousse is. Its dense texture is due to the large quantity of butter it contains. It must be made several hours, or preferably an entire day, in advance.

Procedure

Place the chocolate, coffee, and water in a small saucepan and melt as described on page 29. Stir until very smooth and creamy. Remove from the heat and stir in the butter, piece by piece; then, when all the butter has been incorporated, stir in the egg yolks, one by one. The finished mixture should be very thick and shiny.

Place the egg whites and salt in a large mixing bowl and beat until very stiff. Add the chocolate mixture and fold it in carefully.

Lightly butter the bottom and sides of a 1-quart (1 l) charlotte mold or bowl, then fill it with cold water and immediately pour the water out. This will leave little drops of water here and there on the butter. Fill the mold with the chocolate preparation and place it in the refrigerator to set, from several hours to overnight.

Make the Coffee Custard Sauce and chill as well.

About 30 minutes before serving, turn the marquise out as follows: Fill a bowl with boiling water and set the mold in it for 5 to 10 seconds. Run the blade of a knife all around between the marquise and the edge of the mold, then place a shallow serving dish over the top of the mold and turn everything upside down rapidly. Shake once or twice, then set the platter down on the table. Tap the bottom and sides of the mold with the blade of the knife and lift off the mold. Place the dessert back in the refrigerator so that the surface, which will have melted somewhat, can stiffen again.

To serve, pour enough sauce over the center of the dessert to dribble down the sides and surround it. Place the rest of the sauce in a sauceboat and serve.

Variations

1. Instead of pouring the coffee sauce over the marquise, you may ice the marquise with an icing of your choice and serve the sauce on the side.

2. Decorate the top of the marquise with chocolate shavings and serve with a chocolate sauce instead of a coffee sauce (see photo following p. 56).

INGREDIENTS FOR 4 TO 6 SERVINGS

9 ounces (250 g) semisweet chocolate
2 tablespoons strong coffee
3 tablespoons (50 ml) water
1½ sticks (175 g) butter, cut into 10 pieces and allowed to soften
4 egg yolks
4 egg whites
1 pinch salt
3 cups (700 ml) Coffee Custard Sauce (p. 124)

PREPARATION TIME

40 minutes, plus several hours to set

Chocolate Jelly

CHOCOLAT EN GELÉE

INGREDIENTS FOR 6
SERVINGS

*Generous 1 tablespoon instant
  coffee*
*2 cups (½ l) hot water (for the
  coffee)*
*7 ounces (200 g) semisweet
  chocolate*
*7 tablespoons (85 g) granulated
  sugar*
*1½ tablespoons granulated
  unflavored gelatin softened
  in 4½ tablespoons (65 ml)
  cold water, or 6 sheets
  softened in a bowl of cold
  water*
*Whipped Cream with Grated
  Chocolate (p. 126) or Vanilla
  Custard Sauce (p. 124)*

PREPARATION TIME

*20 to 25 minutes, plus several
hours to set*

M ade without eggs, this dessert has the transparency of a jelly. It should be made a day ahead of time.

Procedure

Mix the instant coffee and the water.

Place the chocolate in a saucepan with 3 tablespoons of the coffee. Melt over low heat as described on page 29, then stir in the sugar. Little by little, add the rest of the coffee and bring to a boil. Allow to simmer for 5 to 6 minutes, stirring constantly.

Remove the saucepan from the heat and add the gelatin (drain sheets if using), stirring until the gelatin has completely melted.

Fill a 3¼-cup (750 ml) bowl with the "jelly." Allow to cool to room temperature, stirring occasionally, then place in the freezer for 3 hours. Finally, transfer the dessert to the refrigerator until the next day.

To turn out, dip the bowl in a larger bowl of boiling water for 3 to 5 seconds. Run the blade of a knife all around between the dessert and the mold, place a serving platter over the top, and turn everything upside down rapidly. Shake a couple of times, place the platter on the table, and lift off the mold. Then place back in the refrigerator until ready to serve.

Serve accompanied by a bowl of Whipped Cream with Grated Chocolate or, if you prefer, Vanilla Custard Sauce, served at room temperature.

Chocolate Pastry Cream

CRÈME PÂTISSIÈRE AU CHOCOLAT

INGREDIENTS FOR 3
CUPS (700 ml)

*5¼ ounces (150 g) bittersweet
  chocolate, broken into pieces*
2 cups (½ l) milk
6 egg yolks
½ cup (100 g) granulated sugar
3 tablespoons (30 g) flour

P astry cream may be made in advance and stored in the refrigerator. It may be eaten like a pudding, accompanied by slices of warm brioche or cookies, or it can be used as a filling for cakes or as a base for other desserts.

Procedure

Place the chocolate and 2 tablespoons of the milk in a small saucepan and melt over low heat. When the chocolate has completely melted, stir in the remaining milk. Bring to a boil, stirring occasionally.

In a medium mixing bowl, beat the egg yolks and sugar until foamy and pale in color. Stir in the flour, then, little by little, the hot chocolate milk.

Pour the mixture back into the saucepan and place over moderate heat. Bring to a boil, stirring constantly; allow to boil for a few seconds, then remove from the heat. The pastry cream should be thick and smooth—if it seems too thick, dilute it with a little chocolate milk. Strain through a fine sieve to remove any lumps and allow to cool, stirring occasionally. When cool, place in the refrigerator, covered, until needed.

Variations

1. Vanilla Pastry Cream: Use 1 vanilla bean split in half lengthwise instead of the chocolate. Place it in the saucepan, add 3 tablespoons (35 g) sugar and the milk, and bring to a boil. Continue as described for Chocolate Pastry Cream, using the same measurements of egg yolks, sugar, and flour, and leaving the vanilla bean in until you strain the cream at the end.

2. Kirsch-Flavored Pastry Cream: Make Vanilla Pastry Cream, then, after straining, stir in 2 tablespoons kirsch.

3. Coffee Pastry Cream: Instead of chocolate, place 2 generous tablespoons instant coffee and 3 tablespoons (35 g) sugar in a saucepan, add the milk, and bring to a boil, stirring. Continue exactly as described for Chocolate Pastry Cream, using the same measurements of egg yolks, sugar, and flour.

PREPARATION TIME

15 to 20 minutes

Chocolate Spice Cream

CRÈME AUX ÉPICES

T his is like a thick custard sauce highly flavored with spices. It may be made in advance and kept in the refrigerator.

Procedure

Place the chocolate and ¼ cup of the milk in a small saucepan and melt over low heat as described on page 29.

Place the rest of the milk and the cinnamon, clove, and vanilla bean in another saucepan. Bring to a boil, remove from the heat, cover, and allow to infuse for 10 minutes, then remove the vanilla bean.

Place the egg yolks and sugar in a mixing bowl and beat until creamy and pale in color.

Little by little, stir the flavored milk into the chocolate. When

INGREDIENTS FOR 6 SERVINGS

7 ounces (200 g) semisweet chocolate
Scant 3¼ cups (¾ l) milk
One 2-inch stick cinnamon
1 clove
1 vanilla bean, split in half lengthwise
8 egg yolks
5 tablespoons (60 g) granulated sugar
Unsweetened cocoa powder

the chocolate has completely dissolved, pour the mixture into the egg-sugar mixture, whisking constantly. Pour everything back into the saucepan used to heat the milk and place over low heat. Heat, stirring constantly, until the cream has thickened enough to coat the spoon lightly. Lift the spoon out of the cream and draw a horizontal line on it with your finger; if the top edge of the line holds its shape, the cream is done. *Do not allow the cream to boil.* Remove from the heat and strain into a bowl.

Allow the cream to cool to room temperature, whisking occasionally, then divide it among individual dessert dishes. Place in the refrigerator until ready to serve.

Just before serving, sift a little cocoa powder over the surface of each one and serve, accompanied by cookies of your choice.

Caramelized Chocolate Custard

CRÈME RENVERSÉE AU CHOCOLAT

INGREDIENTS FOR 6
SERVINGS

*5¼ ounces (150 g) semisweet
    chocolate*
1 quart (1 l) milk
6 whole eggs
*5 tablespoons (60 g) granulated
    sugar*

The Caramel

½ cup (100 g) granulated sugar
2 tablespoons water
5 to 6 drops lemon juice

PREPARATION TIME

*50 to 60 minutes, plus several
hours to set*

A classic French dessert, this custard can also be baked in individual dishes. It may be made up to a day in advance.

Procedure

In a saucepan, melt the chocolate with 3 tablespoons of the milk as described on page 29. Little by little, stir in the rest of the milk, then bring to a boil and allow to simmer for 3 to 4 minutes.

In a mixing bowl, beat the eggs and sugar together until pale in color. Slowly pour the chocolate milk into them, whisking constantly.

Preheat the oven to 400°F (200°C).

Place the sugar and water for the caramel in a 1½-quart (1½ l) charlotte mold. Set the mold over moderate heat and stir until the sugar has dissolved, then stir in the lemon juice. Stop stirring and allow to boil until the sugar begins to change color. Shake the mold over the heat, making the caramel swirl to ensure even coloring. When the caramel is a rich reddish gold color, remove from the heat and turn the mold in all directions to coat the sides completely. This must be done quickly, because the caramel hardens as it cools.

Strain the chocolate mixture into the caramelized mold and place in the middle of the oven to bake for 35 to 40 minutes, or until the blade of a knife inserted in the center of the custard comes out clean. Remove from the oven, allow to cool to room temperature, then place in the refrigerator to set for several hours.

Just before serving, turn the custard out by dipping the mold in very hot water for 1 minute, running the blade of a knife all around between the custard and the edge of the mold, then placing a serving platter on top. Turn everything upside down very quickly and set it on the table with a firm tap. Lift off the mold and serve immediately, with a plate of crisp cookies (vanilla wafers, almond cookies, and so on) on the side.

Michel Guérard's Chocolate Granité

GRANITÉ AU CHOCOLAT AMER DE MICHEL GUÉRARD

T his dessert is made 4 hours in advance, during which time it must be stirred at regular intervals.

Procedure

Place the grated chocolate in a saucepan with 2 tablespoons of the coffee and melt over low heat. When completely melted, stir in the sugar and the rest of the coffee.

Pour the mixture into a shallow dish and allow to cool to room temperature, then place in the freezer. After about an hour, stir the mixture, making sure to scrape the sides of the dish to mix the frozen particles stuck there into the rest. About every 30 minutes, repeat this process, until the entire mixture has crystallized.

To serve, spoon the granité into chilled glasses. Serve with a plate of crisp cookies of your choice.

Note: If you leave the granité too long and it freezes into a block, simply place it in the refrigerator for about 15 to 20 minutes before serving, then break it up with a fork, stir, and serve as described. Ed.

INGREDIENTS FOR 4 SERVINGS

2³/₄ ounces (75 g) bittersweet chocolate, grated
2 cups (½ l) coffee
6 tablespoons (75 g) granulated sugar

PREPARATION TIME

10 to 15 minutes, plus 4 hours in the freezer

Chocolate-Covered Bananas

SUCETTES DE BANANES AU CHOCOLAT

T his is a wonderful thing to make for children. It can be prepared a day ahead of time.

Procedure

Peel the bananas, being careful to remove the "strings," and cut each one in half. Stick a Popsicle stick into the cut end of each one,

INGREDIENTS FOR 12 SERVINGS

6 large ripe bananas
*6 ounces (170 g) bittersweet
    chocolate*
¼ cup (60 ml) water
1 pinch salt
*6½ tablespoons (100 g) butter,
    cut into 6 pieces and softened*
*1 cup (150 g) finely chopped
    hazelnuts (optional)*

PREPARATION TIME

*25 to 30 minutes, plus 1 hour in
the freezer*

lay them on a large platter without touching one another, and place in the freezer for at least 1 hour.

Place the chocolate, water, and salt in a small saucepan and melt over low heat as described on page 29. Stir in the butter, one piece at a time; keep the sauce warm.

Remove the bananas from the freezer.

Spread a large sheet of aluminum foil out on the table. One by one, dip the bananas in the melted chocolate, tipping the saucepan to make the chocolate as deep as possible, and turning the banana in all directions to coat it completely with a thin coat of chocolate. The chocolate will harden as soon as it hits the cold banana. Place the coated banana on the aluminum foil.

The bananas can either be eaten right away or be returned to the freezer to be served another time. In this case, wrap each one separately in aluminum foil first. Remove from the freezer 15 minutes before serving so that they won't be too hard.

If you like, you can make hazelnut-chocolate bananas as follows: Spread the finely chopped nuts out on a sheet of aluminum foil right next to the saucepan of melted chocolate. Dip the bananas in the chocolate as described, then immediately roll them in the nuts before placing them on the large sheet of foil on the table.

Chocolate Ice Cream

GLACE AU CHOCOLAT

Chocolate ice cream is basically a frozen chocolate custard sauce. You must use an ice cream freezer to make it, otherwise it will crystallize and be very grainy.

INGREDIENTS FOR 8 SERVINGS

*7 ounces (200 g) semisweet
    chocolate*
1 pinch salt
1 quart (1 l) milk
8 egg yolks
*7 tablespoons (90 g) granulated
    sugar*

PREPARATION TIME

*20 to 25 minutes plus about 3
hours cooling and freezing time*

Procedure

Place the chocolate, salt, and ¼ cup (60 ml) of milk in a saucepan and melt over low heat as described on page 29. Slowly stir in the rest of the milk, bring just to a boil, and allow to simmer for 3 to 4 minutes. Remove from the heat.

In a mixing bowl, beat the egg yolks and sugar together until foamy and pale in color. Little by little, add the chocolate milk, then pour back into the saucepan and place over low heat. Cook, stirring constantly, until thick enough to coat a wooden spoon lightly and until a horizontal line drawn in the cream on the spoon holds its shape. *Do not allow to boil.*

Remove from the heat and pour into a mixing bowl to cool. Allow to cool to room temperature, whisking from time to time to make the cream light and foamy. Then pour into the canister of an ice cream freezer and freeze until the mixture is the consistency of ice cream. Remove the churning paddle and either place the canister of ice cream in a deep freezer or pour into a mold and place in the freezer.

About 20 to 30 minutes before serving, move the ice cream from the freezer to the refrigerator so it won't be too hard. Scoop it and pile it in a dome in the center of individual dessert plates, surrounded by one of the following sauces: Coffee Custard Sauce (p. 124), Vanilla Custard Sauce (p. 124), Chocolate Custard Sauce (p. 123), or Whipped Cream with Melted Chocolate (p. 125). Serve with cookies.

Chocolate Parfait

PARFAIT AU CHOCOLAT

INGREDIENTS FOR 6 SERVINGS

4 1/4 ounces (125 g) semisweet chocolate
3 tablespoons (50 ml) water
3 tablespoons (35 g) granulated sugar
3 egg yolks
2 teaspoons vanilla sugar (see note to Whipped Cream with Melted Chocolate, p. 125)
1/2 pint (240 ml) heavy (whipping) cream, chilled
Hot Fudge Sauce (p. 123) (optional)

PREPARATION TIME

25 to 30 minutes, plus freezing time

I n France, the word *parfait* refers to a very rich ice cream made with whipped cream and frozen in the freezer. It must be made a day in advance.

Although not necessary, Hot Fudge Sauce (p. 123) is absolutely delicious with this parfait.

Procedure

Place the chocolate and water in a saucepan and melt over low heat as described on page 29. Add the sugar and stir until it has melted.

Remove the saucepan from the heat and stir in the egg yolks, one by one, then place the saucepan in the refrigerator to cool.

Add the vanilla sugar to the cream and whip until soft peaks are formed. Remove the chocolate from the refrigerator, stir, and fold it into the whipped cream. Transfer the mixture to a clean bowl or mold and place in the freezer until the next day.

Serve in any one of the following ways:

1. About 1 hour before serving, turn the parfait out onto a serving platter (dip the mold into hot water for a few seconds, run the blade of a knife around between the parfait and the mold, place the platter over it, and turn everything upside down). Place the platter back in the freezer so that the melted edges can set again. Then 15 minutes before serving, transfer the parfait to the refrigerator so that it won't be too cold.

2. Spoon the parfait out of the bowl and mound it in the center of individual dessert plates, pour Hot Fudge Sauce around it, and serve.

3. Scoop the parfait into glasses and pour Hot Fudge Sauce over it to make a sundae; when the sauce hits the cold parfait, it will thicken to an almost caramel consistency.

Frozen Chocolate Soufflé with Rum Tidbits

SOUFFLÉ GLACÉ AU CHOCOLAT, AUX PETITS DÉS PARFUMÉS

INGREDIENTS FOR 6 SERVINGS

5 lady fingers
2 tablespoons light rum
Chocolate Parfait (p. 41)
½ pint (240 ml) heavy (whipping) cream
4¼ ounces (125 g) semisweet chocolate
3 tablespoons (50 ml) water
3 tablespoons (35 g) granulated sugar
3 egg yolks
2 teaspoons vanilla sugar (see note to Whipped Cream with Melted Chocolate, p. 125)
Unsweetened cocoa powder

PREPARATION TIME

35 to 40 minutes, plus freezing time

T his dessert should be made either a day in advance or in the morning for the evening.

Procedure

Take a soufflé mold about 5½ inches (14 cm) in diameter. Cut a band of thin cardboard long enough to encircle the mold completely and 4 inches (10 cm) high (see note). Tie or tape it around the mold so that it extends about 1½ inches (4 cm) above the edge. Place the mold in the refrigerator.

Cut the lady fingers into tiny cubes. Spread them out on a cutting board or sheet of aluminum foil and sprinkle the rum over them, using a pastry brush.

Make the Chocolate Parfait, then fold in the rum-flavored cubes, being careful to distribute the cubes evenly throughout the parfait and working gently to avoid breaking them.

Remove the soufflé mold from the refrigerator and fill with the parfait; it should come close to the top of the cardboard band. Shake gently to level the parfait, then place in the freezer to harden for several hours.

About 30 minutes before serving, remove the soufflé from the freezer, sprinkle the top with cocoa powder as described on page 117, then untie or untape the cardboard and carefully peel it off. Like a baked soufflé, the frozen soufflé will extend above the edge of the mold. Place in the refrigerator for the remainder of the 30 minutes to allow the parfait to soften slightly before serving.

Note: In place of thin cardboard, a sheet of aluminum foil long enough to go around the mold and folded over on itself several times to make it more rigid may be used instead. Ed.

2

Cakes · Tarts Puff Pastries and Profiteroles

Chocolate, Almond, and Orange Tart (*Tarte de chocolat, aux amandes et aux oranges*), p. 59

Chocolate-Hazelnut-Coffee Tart (*Tarte de chocolat, aux noisettes et au café*), p. 60

Coconut-Chocolate Tart (*Tarte à la noix de coco et au chocolat*), p. 61

Chocolate-Walnut Tart (*Tarte au chocolat et aux noix*), p. 62

Monsieur Robert's Chocolate Tart with Pears (*La tarte chocolatée de M. Robert à la crème et aux poires*), p. 63

Chocolate-Caramel Quiche (*Quiche de chocolat au caramel*), p. 64

PUFF PASTRIES

Puff Pastry (*La pâte feuilletée*), p. 66

To Cut and Bake Puff Pastry (*Préparation et cuisson des feuilletés*), p. 67

Whipped-Cream Pastries with Caramel Custard Sauce (*Feuilletés de Chantilly de chocolat à la crème caramel*), p. 68

Chocolate Pastries with Coffee Custard Sauce (*Feuilletés de chocolat à la crème au café*), p. 69

Kirsch-Flavored Pastries with Two Sauces (*Feuilletés de crème au kirsch aux deux sauces*), p. 69

Frangipane Pastries with Pears and Chocolate Sauce (*Feuilletés de frangipane aux poires, à la sauce au chocolat*), p. 70

Pastries with Chocolate Mousse and Oranges (*Feuilletés de mousse de chocolat aux oranges*), p. 71

PROFITEROLES

Cream Puff Pastry (*La pâte à choux*), p. 72

Chocolate Profiteroles with Vanilla Sauce (*Profiteroles de glace au chocolat à la crème à la vanille*), p. 73

Vanilla Profiteroles with Hot Chocolate Sauce (*Profiteroles de glace à la vanille, sauce chocolat*), p. 73

Hazelnut Profiteroles with Hot Fudge Sauce (Profiteroles de glace à la noisette et à la hot fudge sauce), p. 74

Pistachio Profiteroles with Honey-Flavored Chocolate Sauce (Profiteroles de glace à la pistache à la sauce chocolat au miel), p. 74

Passion Fruit Profiteroles with Bananas and Chocolate Sauce (Profiteroles exotiques au chocolat), p. 75

There are four types of recipes in this chapter, but they fall roughly into two categories: The cakes and tarts can be used in a variety of ways—as desserts at the end of a dinner, as an accompaniment to tea or coffee in the afternoon, or as part of a combination dessert. Their great advantage is that they can be made in advance, sometimes up to a day in advance, which makes the planning of a dinner much easier.

Puff pastries and profiteroles, on the other hand, are more elegant desserts, destined to be served at more formal dinners. Although their various elements may be made in advance, they must be put together at the last minute and for this reason tend to be reserved for special occasions.

Don't hesitate to experiment with combinations of your own; the ideas presented in this chapter are only a few of the possibilities.

Chocolate-Apricot Layer Cake

BISCUIT AU CHOCOLAT ET À L'ABRICOT

The cake batter may be baked up to several days in advance; it keeps fresh if wrapped tightly in aluminum foil. The cake should be filled and iced the day it is to be served, but it will keep for 2 to 3 hours in a cool place.

Procedure

To make the cake: Preheat the oven to 350°F (175°C).

In a mixing bowl, beat the egg yolks and sugar until pale in color and thick and creamy in texture.

Mix the flour and cocoa together with a fork to eliminate any lumps; the color should be uniform when thoroughly mixed. Stir the egg-sugar mixture into the flour-cocoa mixture.

INGREDIENTS FOR 8 SERVINGS

The Batter

5 egg yolks
⅔ cup (125 g) granulated sugar
9 tablespoons (90 g) flour
¼ cup (40 g) unsweetened cocoa powder
4 egg whites
6 tablespoons (90 g) butter, melted

The Filling and the Icing

½ cup (125 ml) Chocolate
    Butter Cream (p. 125)
Apricot jam (about ½ jar)
Simple Chocolate Icing (p. 115)

PREPARATION TIME

*The cake—1 to 1¼ hours; the
filling, icing, and assembling—
30 to 35 minutes*

In a separate mixing bowl, beat the egg whites until stiff, then fold the chocolate mixture into them. Fold in the melted butter; when done, the mixture should be of uniform color and texture. ·

Butter and flour a 1-quart (1 l) charlotte mold. Pour in the batter (the mold should be ⅔ to ¾ full) and bake for 45 minutes to 1 hour, or until the blade of a knife inserted in the center comes out clean.

Remove from the oven, allow to cool for 5 to 10 minutes, then turn out onto a cardboard base cut to the size of the cake. Set on a cake rack or pastry board to cool completely.

To fill and ice: Make the Chocolate Butter Cream.

Cut the cake horizontally into 3 equal layers, using a long, serrated knife.

Spread a layer of butter cream on the bottom layer, set the middle layer on top, and spread it with apricot jam. Set the top layer in place and spread it with a very thin layer of apricot jam.

Make the Simple Chocolate Icing. When it has cooled to warm and thickened enough to spread without running too much, ice the cake completely as described on page 114.

Allow the icing to cool and set completely, then slide a flexible-blade metal spatula under the cardboard base and transfer the cake to a serving platter.

Chocolate-Almond Cake

BISCUIT D'AMANDES AU CHOCOLAT

The cake batter may be baked well in advance and kept wrapped in plastic in the refrigerator. The cake should be filled and iced the day it is to be eaten, but it will keep for 2 to 3 hours in a cool place.

Procedure

Preheat the oven to 325°F (165°C).

In a mixing bowl, mix the sugar and ground almonds together, then stir in the egg yolks. Beat the mixture vigorously to make it creamy and light. Little by little, beat in the coconut, cocoa, and whole egg; mix well.

In a separate bowl, beat the egg whites until stiff. Begin folding them into the almond–egg yolk mixture, sprinkling in the flour ⅓ at a time as you do so. Lastly, fold in the melted butter.

Butter a 1½-quart (1½ l) charlotte mold. Pour in the batter and bake for 40 to 45 minutes, or until the blade of a knife inserted in the center comes out clean.

Remove from the oven and allow to cool for 15 minutes, or until warm. A point probably formed in the center of the cake while it was baking—if this point has not sunk down after 15 minutes' cooling, slice it off to make it even with the rest. Turn the cake out onto a pastry board or cake rack and allow to cool completely.

To make the filling: The filling must be made enough in advance to be able to cool completely.

Place the chocolate and water in a small saucepan and melt over low heat as described on page 29. Stir in the *crème fraîche* or heavy cream.

In a mixing bowl, beat the egg yolks and sugar until pale in color and very thick and creamy. Stir in the chocolate mixture. In a small bowl, dilute the cornstarch with the milk, stir into the chocolate mixture, and pour into a saucepan. Place over moderately low heat and bring to a boil, stirring constantly, then lower the heat and cook, still stirring, until the cream has darkened in color and become thick and smooth (about 1 minute). Remove from the heat and allow to cool, stirring frequently, then stir in the rum.

To ice the cake: Make the Small Chocolate Shavings.

Make the Simple Chocolate Icing; be sure you keep it warm as you proceed.

Cut the cake horizontally into 3 equal layers. Place the bottom layer on a cardboard base of the same size. Spread it with about half of the filling. Cover with the second layer, spread with filling, and cover with the top layer. Scrape off any filling that bulges out from between the layers, then ice the cake as described on page 114. Allow the icing to set a little, then sprinkle the top with the chocolate shavings.

When the icing has set completely, slide a flexible-blade metal spatula under the cardboard base and transfer the cake to a serving platter.

INGREDIENTS FOR 8 SERVINGS

The Cake

⅔ cup (125 g) granulated sugar
Scant ⅔ cup (75 g) ground almonds
6 egg yolks
½ cup (40 g) dried grated coconut
5 tablespoons (50 g) unsweetened cocoa powder
1 whole egg
6 egg whites
¾ cup (100 g) flour
6½ tablespoons (100 g) butter, melted

The Filling

2½ ounces (70 g) semisweet chocolate
2 tablespoons water
¾ cup (200 ml) crème fraîche (p. 30) or heavy cream
5 egg yolks
¾ cup (150 g) granulated sugar
2 teaspoons cornstarch
2 tablespoons milk
1 teaspoon dark rum

The Icing

Small Chocolate Shavings (p. 117)
Simple Chocolate Icing (p. 115)

PREPARATION TIME

The cake—1 hour to 1 hour 20 minutes; the filling—20 to 25 minutes

Chocolate Charlotte

CHARLOTTE AU CHOCOLAT

INGREDIENTS FOR 8 SERVINGS

14 ounces (400 g) semisweet chocolate

2¼ sticks (250 g) butter, cut into 15 pieces and allowed to soften

5 egg yolks

7 tablespoons (85 g) granulated sugar

5 egg whites

1 pinch salt

½ cup (120 ml) Grand Marnier liqueur

½ cup (120 ml) water

30 lady fingers

The Orange Sauce

1⅓ cups (300 ml) freshly squeezed orange juice

1 cup (200 g) granulated sugar

Simple Chocolate Icing (p. 115)

PREPARATION TIME

The charlotte—45 minutes; the sauce—5 to 10 minutes; the icing—6 to 7 minutes

T his dessert should be made half a day to a day in advance.

Procedure

Melt the chocolate in a double boiler as described on page 29. Remove from the heat and stir in the butter, piece by piece. Allow to cool, stirring occasionally, until the mixture is as thick as mayonnaise.

Beat the egg yolks and sugar together until pale in color and thick and creamy. Stir carefully into the chocolate.

Place the egg whites and salt in a separate mixing bowl and beat until very stiff. Fold the chocolate mixture into the egg whites until uniform in color and texture. Set aside.

Mix the Grand Marnier and water together in a soup plate. Dip the flat (bottom) side of each lady finger into this mixture for a second or two; the lady fingers should be moistened, but not so wet as to fall apart. If you run out of the Grand Marnier mixture, make more. Spread the moistened lady fingers out upside down.

Line the bottom of the charlotte mold with lady fingers, trimming them so that they will fit into the circular shape; place them in the mold upside down. Line the sides of the mold with vertically placed lady fingers, the rounded side against the mold. Make sure they fit tightly into the mold.

Fill the mold with the chocolate mixture prepared earlier. Cover with a layer of lady fingers, rounded side down. If the lady fingers lining the side of the mold extend above those covering the filling, cut them off to make the surface even. Place the charlotte in the refrigerator to set for at least 3 hours.

To make the Orange Sauce: Place the orange juice and sugar in a blender and blend for about 30 seconds to melt the sugar. Strain into a bowl, pressing any solids left in the strainer to extract all the juice. Place in the refrigerator.

To serve: Remove the orange sauce from the refrigerator; it's better at room temperature.

Turn out the charlotte by running the blade of a knife all around the edge to detach any lady fingers that might be sticking to the mold. Place a serving platter over the top of the mold and turn everything upside down. Shake to loosen the mold and lift it off. Return the charlotte to the refrigerator.

Make the Simple Chocolate Icing, then ice the charlotte as described on page 114; wipe the platter clean around the charlotte. Spoon a ring of orange sauce around the dessert and serve, with the rest of the sauce in a sauceboat.

Mama's Cake

GÂTEAU DE MAMAN

T his cake should be made a day ahead of time.

Procedure

Make the Chocolate Mousse; set aside.

To make the dipping liquid: In a mixing bowl, mix together the instant coffee and hot water. Stir in the sugar; when it has melted, stir in the rum. Keep this mixture warm (it will be used for dipping the cookies, so if you run out, make more).

Pour some of the dipping liquid into a soup plate. One by one, dip 12 of the cookies into it just long enough to flavor them but not make them soggy. Arrange them in a rectangle on a rectangular serving platter (3 rows of 4 cookies each) making sure that there are no spaces between them. Sprinkle a little of the liquid over them with a spoon.

With a flexible-blade metal spatula, spread ¼ of the mousse over the layer of cookies. Cover the mousse with a second layer of cookies dipped, arranged, and sprinkled exactly like the first. Spread with mousse again and continue until you have made 4 layers of cookies and 4 layers of mousse (the top layer will be of mousse). Smooth the sides of the cake with the tip of the spatula so that they are nice and neat and the alternating layers are clearly visible.

With a paper towel clean off any mousse or dipping liquid that might have dripped onto the platter, then place the cake in the refrigerator for 24 hours. Just before serving, sprinkle with cocoa powder (don't forget to wipe off any cocoa that falls on the platter before you take it to the table).

Comment: This cake will keep very well for 2 to 3 days in the refrigerator; in fact it tastes even better then.

INGREDIENTS FOR 10 SERVINGS

Double recipe Chocolate Mousse (p. 32)

The Dipping Liquid

2 teaspoons instant coffee
1 cup (¼ l) water, heated
¼ cup (50 g) granulated sugar
4 teaspoons dark rum

48 rectangular butter cookies (French "Petit beurre Lu," shortbread, or any other hard, plain cookie)
Unsweetened cocoa powder

PREPARATION TIME

Mousse—30 to 35 minutes; cake —35 to 40 minutes

Mother Guérard's Cake

GÂTEAU DE MAMAN GUÉRARD

INGREDIENTS FOR 8 SERVINGS

10 ounces (280 g) semisweet chocolate
2½ sticks (280 g) butter, cut into 20 pieces
9 egg yolks
1⅓ cups (280 g) granulated sugar
5 egg whites
1 pinch salt

Unsweetened cocoa powder (optional)
Browned slivered almonds (optional)

PREPARATION TIME

1¼ to 1½ hours

The cake may be baked a day in advance, then iced with the mousse an hour or two before serving.

Procedure

Preheat the oven to 300°F (150°C).

Melt the chocolate in a double boiler as described on page 29. Remove from the heat and stir in the butter, one piece at a time. The finished mixture should be very thick and creamy.

In a mixing bowl, beat the egg yolks and sugar until pale in color and very thick. Add the chocolate, beating until a uniform color is obtained.

In a separate mixing bowl, beat the egg whites and salt together until very stiff, then add the chocolate mixture and carefully fold it in until uniform in color and texture.

Pour about ¾ of the batter into a buttered rectangular 8-by-12-inch (20 × 30 cm) cake pan, then bake in the middle of the oven for 45 minutes to 1 hour. Reserve the rest of the batter (really a mousse) in the refrigerator.

When the cake is done, it should have risen considerably and be dry and cracked on top but still very creamy in the middle. Remove from the oven, allow to cool for about 5 minutes, then run the tip of the knife all around it and turn it out. Leave it upside down to cool completely.

When cool, ice the cake with the remaining mousse to cover the top and sides, smoothing it with a flexible-blade metal spatula. Place in the refrigerator for at least 30 minutes so that the mousse can set again.

To serve: Either serve the cake as it is, or, if you want a more "refined" presentation, sprinkle with cocoa powder or browned slivered almonds as described on pages 117 and 118.

Sylvie's Cake

GÂTEAU DE SYLVIE

Y ou can either make this cake in advance and eat it cold or bake it during the meal and eat it warm.

Procedure

Make the Coffee or Vanilla Custard Sauce well in advance so that it will have time to cool.

Preheat the oven to 300°F (150°C).

In a medium saucepan, dissolve the instant coffee in the water, then add the chocolate and melt over low heat as described on page 29. Remove from the heat and stir in the butter, piece by piece.

One by one, stir in the egg yolks, then the flour and sugar, and finally the rum.

Place the egg whites and salt in a mixing bowl and beat until very stiff. Carefully fold in the chocolate mixture, then pour the batter into a buttered rectangular 8-by-12-inch (20 × 30 cm) baking dish. If the cake is to be eaten warm, use an ovenproof dish it can be served in.

Place the cake in the oven and bake for about 20 minutes. Although it should look dry on top, the cake should be "undercooked": the blade of a knife inserted in the center should come out almost clean, but not quite.

If served warm, leave the cake in the dish and serve a sauceboat of custard sauce on the side.

If served cold, it can be turned out once it has cooled completely. Run the tip of a knife all around between the cake and the mold. With a spatula, lift up the edge of the cake on all sides to loosen it and let a little air in underneath. Place a platter over the mold and turn everything upside down. Set the platter down on the table with a bang to make the cake fall onto it and lift off the mold.

Cut the cake into squares, place one in the center of each dessert plate, spoon a little of the sauce around it and serve, with the rest of the sauce in a sauceboat.

INGREDIENTS FOR 8 SERVINGS

Coffee or Vanilla Custard Sauce (p. 124)
1 teaspoon instant coffee
¼ cup (60 ml) water, warmed
10½ ounces (300 g) semisweet chocolate
8½ tablespoons (125 g) butter, cut into 8 pieces and allowed to soften
4 egg yolks
1 tablespoon flour
1 tablespoon granulated sugar
1 teaspoon rum
4 egg whites
1 pinch salt

PREPARATION TIME

30 to 40 minutes

Sylvie's Layer Cake

GÂTEAU FOURRÉ DE SYLVIE

INGREDIENTS FOR 10 SERVINGS

10 ½ ounces (300 g) semisweet chocolate

5 tablespoons (75 ml) water

8 ½ tablespoons (125 g) butter, cut into 8 pieces and allowed to soften

4 egg yolks

2 tablespoons flour

1 tablespoon granulated sugar

4 egg whites

1 pinch salt

The Filling and the Icing

½ cup (125 ml) Chocolate Butter Cream (p. 125)

2 teaspoons vanilla sugar (see note to Whipped Cream with Melted Chocolate, p. 125)

6 ½ tablespoons (100 ml) heavy (whipping) cream, chilled

Simple Chocolate Icing (p. 115)

PREPARATION TIME

The cake—50 to 60 minutes; the filling and icing—35 to 40 minutes

T he cake may be baked a day in advance, then filled and iced the day it is to be served.

Procedure

Preheat the oven to 350°F (175°C).

Butter an 8-inch (20 cm) loaf pan.

Place the chocolate and water in a medium saucepan and melt as described on page 29. Remove from the heat and stir in the butter, piece by piece.

One by one, stir in the egg yolks, then the flour, and finally the sugar.

Place the egg whites and salt in a mixing bowl and beat until very stiff. Carefully fold in the chocolate mixture, then pour the batter into the buttered mold and place in the middle of the oven to bake for about 1 hour, or until the blade of a knife inserted in the center comes out clean. Remove from the oven and allow to cool.

To fill and ice the cake: Make the Chocolate Butter Cream and leave it at room temperature.

Add the vanilla sugar to the cream and beat until it forms soft peaks.

Cut a piece of cardboard exactly the size of the top of the mold. Run the blade of a knife all around between the cake and the edge of the mold, then place the cardboard over the top and turn everything upside down. Place on a pastry board and lift off the mold.

Using a serrated knife, cut the cake horizontally into 3 equal layers. On the bottom layer, spread all but about 2 tablespoons of the butter cream. Set the middle layer of cake in place and cover it with the whipped cream. Set the top layer in place and spread it with the remaining butter cream.

Make the Simple Chocolate Icing. Allow to cool to lukewarm and thicken slightly. Ice the cake on the top and sides as described on page 114, then place in the refrigerator so that the icing can set. Transfer to a serving platter and serve.

Comment: For a nice decorative touch, Small Chocolate Shavings (p. 117) may be arranged on top of the cake before the icing has set.

Pierre Vandenameele's Cake

LE GÂTEAU DE PIERRE VANDENAMEELE

T his cake is a specialty of Pierre Vandenameele, chef of La Poularde, a restaurant in Houdan, just west of Paris.

The first day, bake the cake and make the chocolate mousse. The second, make the whipped cream, fill the cake, and, if you like, ice it.

Procedure

To make the cake: The day before you plan to serve it, preheat the oven to 350°F (175°C).

Line the bottom of a rectangular cake pan 8 by 12 inches (20 × 30 cm) and about ¾ inch (2 cm) high, with a sheet of parchment paper. Butter and flour the sides of the pan and the paper.

Sift the flour and cocoa powder into a bowl, then mix together if necessary with a fork in order to obtain a uniform color.

In a mixing bowl, beat the eggs and sugar with an electric mixer at medium speed until almost white in color and almost the consistency of whipped cream. Sprinkle in the flour-cocoa mixture and continue beating until it is of uniform color.

Pour the batter into the cake pan, spreading it out to an even thickness, about ½ inch (1.2 cm), with a flexible-blade metal spatula. Bake for about 20 minutes, or until the cake begins to resist when you press on it lightly.

Remove the cake from the oven and run the tip of a knife all around the sides to loosen it from the mold. Place a clean dish towel over the cake, set a cake rack upside down over that, then turn everything over. Lift off the cake pan, then carefully peel off the parchment paper (if the paper sticks at all, brush it lightly with water, wait a minute or two, then peel it off). Cover the cake with a second dish towel and allow to cool completely; then cover tightly with aluminum foil, and leave overnight.

To make the mousse: Melt the chocolate in a double boiler as described on page 29. Once it has been stirred and is perfectly smooth, remove from the heat and stir in the butter, piece by piece. One by one, stir in the egg yolks, then continue stirring until the mixture is as thick as mayonnaise.

In a small saucepan, melt the ½ ounce (15 g) chocolate over very low heat.

In a large mixing bowl, beat the egg whites until thick and foamy, add the sugar, and continue beating until very stiff and shiny. Fold in the melted chocolate from the saucepan, then the chocolate mixture prepared earlier. When the mousse is of uniform

INGREDIENTS FOR 8 SERVINGS

The Cake

6 tablespoons (60 g) flour
1½ tablespoons (15 g) unsweetened cocoa powder
4 whole eggs
½ cup (100 g) granulated sugar

The Mousse

2¼ ounces (65 g) semisweet chocolate, broken into pieces
3 tablespoons (45 g) butter, cut into 3 pieces and allowed to soften
1 egg yolk
½ ounce (15 g) semisweet chocolate (for the egg whites)
2 egg whites
3 tablespoons (40 g) granulated sugar

The Syrup

3 tablespoons (50 ml) water
¼ cup (50 g) granulated sugar
2 tablespoons rum

The Whipped Cream

½ teaspoon granulated unflavored gelatin softened in 1½ teaspoons cold water, or ½ sheet softened in a bowl of cold water
1 teaspoon boiling water
½ cup (125 ml) heavy (whipping) cream, chilled
1½ teaspoons instant coffee

The Icing (optional)

2 ounces (60 g) semisweet chocolate
1 tablespoon water

The cake—40 to 45 minutes;
the fillings—25 minutes;
assembling the cake—30 to 35
minutes, plus at least 1 hour
refrigeration

color and texture, place it, covered, in the refrigerator until the next day.

To make the syrup: On the day you plan to serve the cake, first make the sugar syrup by putting the water and sugar in a small saucepan, bringing it to a full boil, and removing it from the heat. Allow to cool to warm, then add the rum.

To make the whipped cream: Place the heavy cream in a mixing bowl in the refrigerator. If using the sheet gelatin, drain it. Dissolve the softened gelatin in the boiling water.

Add the instant coffee to the chilled heavy cream. Beat with an electric mixer at medium speed. When the coffee has dissolved, add the gelatin and continue beating until the cream forms soft peaks.

To assemble the cake: Uncover the cake and cut it crosswise into 3 equal rectangles. Prepare 2 pastry bags, each with a ⅝-inch (15 mm) nozzle; fill one with the mousse, the other with the whipped cream.

Place one of the pieces of cake on a serving platter. Brush it generously with syrup, then apply 3 thick rows of chocolate mousse lengthwise, spaced equally apart. Fill the 2 spaces between them with the whipped cream.

Place a second piece of cake on top, pressing it down lightly. Brush it generously with syrup, then apply the whipped cream and mousse in the opposite order, that is, 3 lines of whipped cream and 2 of mousse. Set the third piece of cake on top, press lightly, then smooth any of the filling that may be bulging out from between the layers. Brush the top layer of cake generously with syrup, then place the cake in the refrigerator for at least 1 hour, preferably more. (The cake must be very cold in order to be sliced correctly, so the refrigerator must be on the coldest possible setting.)

To slice the cake, take a sharp knife, dip it in hot water, then wipe it dry; this will help you to cut nice, even slices.

To make the icing: If you like, you may ice the cake just before serving by melting the chocolate with the water over low heat. Stir until smooth and creamy, then pour onto the top of the cake as it comes from the refrigerator and spread it out rapidly with a flexible-blade metal spatula (do *not* ice the sides of the cake); the chocolate will harden almost immediately. Slice the cake as described above.

Variations

Although this cake is normally served plain, it may also be served with a sauce, as shown in the photo. Make a Coffee Custard Sauce (p. 124) and allow to cool completely. Cover the bottom of each plate with it, swirl in some melted chocolate, place a slice of cake on it, and serve.

Rolled Cake with Chocolate Mousse

ROULÉ DE MOUSSE AU CHOCOLAT

T his cake keeps well in the refrigerator, so it can be made up to a day in advance.

Procedure

Make the Chocolate Mousse in advance so that it has time to chill and set.

Preheat the oven to 425°F (220°C).

In a mixing bowl, beat the egg yolks and sugar until very pale in color and very thick (almost like whipped cream). Sprinkle in the flour and beat just long enough to mix it in.

In a separate mixing bowl, beat the egg whites and salt until very stiff. Fold ½ the whites and all of the melted butter into the egg yolk–flour mixture, then fold in the remaining whites.

Butter a sheet of parchment paper and line a baking sheet with it. Spread the batter into a rectangle about 8½ by 12½ inches (22 × 32 cm) and approximately ¼ inch (½ cm) thick all over. Bake for 8 to 10 minutes, or until the surface has begun to brown and begins to resist to the touch when pressed lightly.

Remove from the oven and turn upside down onto a dish towel placed on a pastry board (since the cake is stuck to the paper, simply lift it off the baking sheet with the paper). Peel off the paper; if it sticks at all, lightly moisten the paper by brushing it with water, wait about 2 minutes, then peel it off. Cover the cake with a second dish towel and allow to cool completely.

When the cake is cold, remove the towels and trim the edges of the cake to make a neat rectangle. Remove the mousse from the refrigerator and spread it all over, leaving about ½ inch (1 cm) of cake uncovered at the end you will be rolling toward. Roll the cake up (crosswise), then roll it in some cocoa powder that has been poured onto a long platter. The cake should be well coated all over with the cocoa.

Place the finished cake on a rectangular serving platter with the fold on the bottom. Blow off any excess cocoa powder, then chill until ready to serve. If necessary, just before serving cut off the ends with a serrated knife to make them nice and neat.

INGREDIENTS FOR 6
TO 8 SERVINGS

½ recipe Chocolate Mousse (p. 32)
3 egg yolks
⅓ cup (60 g) granulated sugar
6 tablespoons (60 g) flour
2 egg whites
1 pinch salt
1½ tablespoons (20 g) butter, melted
Unsweetened cocoa powder

PREPARATION TIME

25 to 30 minutes, plus time to cool (about 30 minutes)

Chestnut Cake

GÂTEAU AUX MARRONS

INGREDIENTS FOR 6 TO 8 SERVINGS

1¼ sticks (150 g) butter, softened
½ cup (100 g) granulated sugar
3½ ounces (100 g) semisweet chocolate
1 tablespoon water
1 pinch salt
14 ounces (400 g) canned whole chestnuts
2 cups (½ l) milk, heated
Unsweetened cocoa powder
Hot Chocolate Sauce (p. 120)

PREPARATION TIME

The cake—40 to 45 minutes; the sauce—8 to 10 minutes, plus refrigeration time

T he cake should be made a day in advance, then sprinkled with cocoa the day it is to be eaten. The sauce should be made at the last minute.

Procedure

Place the butter and sugar in a mixing bowl and mix, first with a fork, then with a wooden spoon, until smooth and creamy; reserve.

Place the chocolate, water, and salt in a saucepan. Melt over low heat, stirring until smooth and creamy.

Drain the chestnuts and puree them in a food processor; add the hot milk little by little to make a smooth, thick puree. Add the melted chocolate and process to mix it in, then finally add the butter-sugar mixture. The final mixture should be very smooth, creamy, and of uniform color.

Line an 8-inch (20 cm) loaf pan with aluminum foil; the foil should extend well beyond the edges of the mold. Roll the edges of the foil around the edge of the mold.

Pour the batter into the mold and tap it hard against the table to even it out and make sure there are no air holes. Place in the refrigerator overnight.

The next day, remove the cake from the refrigerator and turn it out onto a serving platter; peel off the aluminum foil. Sprinkle with cocoa powder as described on page 117, then return it to the refrigerator until ready to serve.

Serve with a sauceboat of Hot Chocolate Sauce.

Chocolate Sponge Cake

SPONGE-CAKE AU CHOCOLAT

T his cake will keep for several days. It can be eaten either plain or garnished with fruits, and so on.

Procedure

Preheat the oven to 350°F (175°C).

Butter an 8-inch (20 cm) loaf pan.

Place the egg yolk, whole eggs, sugar, and vanilla extract in a saucepan and stir over low heat until hot to the touch. Transfer to

Chocolate Marquise with Coffee Sauce (page 35)

Chocolate Parfait (page 41)

Pierre Vandenameele's Cake (page 53)

Some Tarts (pages 59–61)

a warm mixing bowl and beat with an electric mixer at moderate speed until the mixture has quadrupled in volume and become as thick as whipped cream (about 5 minutes).

Mix the flour, cocoa powder, and salt together with a fork to eliminate lumps; the mixture should be of uniform color. Using your hand to mix with, fold the flour-cocoa mixture into the egg mixture, ⅓ at a time, until the mixture feels perfectly homogenous in texture and is of uniform color. Fold the melted butter into the batter, then pour it into the mold, tapping the mold lightly against the table to make sure the batter is evenly distributed.

Bake for 25 to 30 minutes, or until the blade of a knife inserted in the center of the cake comes out clean and dry. Remove from the oven and allow to cool for about 5 minutes, or until the cake has shrunk from the sides of the mold. Then turn out and allow to cool right side up before serving.

INGREDIENTS FOR 6 to 8 SERVINGS

1 egg yolk
4 whole eggs
⅔ cup (120 g) granulated sugar
½ teaspoon vanilla extract
6 tablespoons (60 g) flour
6 tablespoons (60 g) unsweetened cocoa powder
1 pinch salt
2 tablespoons butter, melted

PREPARATION TIME

40 to 50 minutes

TARTS

S ome of the following tarts have special pastry bottoms. These are included with the recipe. Others simply use traditional types of dough. You can either use commercial, ready-to-bake piecrusts or make your own. For those who prefer the homemade variety, here are two recipes.

Short Pastry Dough

LA PÂTE BRISÉE

I t's best to make this dough the night before you need it. It will keep for 1 week in the refrigerator if tightly wrapped in plastic.

Procedure

Place the flour on the table and make a well in the center of it. Sprinkle the powdered milk, sugar, and salt over it. Break the egg into the well. Begin adding the butter, piece by piece, and mixing it into the flour by stirring with your finger. With your other hand brush the flour into the well from the edges; when the mixture in the well begins to thicken into a dough, mix in the remainder of the flour with both hands, using a pinching motion.

INGREDIENTS FOR 1 POUND 1½ OUNCES (500 g) DOUGH

1¾ cups (250 g) flour
¼ cup (20 g) powdered milk
2 teaspoons granulated sugar
1 teaspoon salt
1 whole egg
1½ sticks (175 g) butter, cut into 8 pieces and allowed to soften.
2 teaspoons cold water

PREPARATION TIME

*15 minutes, plus refrigeration
time and 25 to 30 minutes to
bake*

Sprinkle the water over the dough and continue pinching; as the dough begins to stick together, form it into a ball. *Fraiser* or "knead" the dough once by pushing bits of it against the table and away from you with the heel of your hand. Gather the dough up, form it into a ball, place it in a plastic bag, and chill it in the refrigerator until the next day.

About 30 minutes before rolling the dough out, remove it from the refrigerator.

Preheat the oven to 450°F (235°C).

Roll the dough out on a lightly floured table to a thickness of about ¼ inch (5 mm).

Line a 9- to 10-inch (23 to 25 cm) pie pan with a removable bottom (or a springform cake pan) with the dough. Pinch the edges to form a border and prick the bottom all over with the prongs of a fork. Line the dough with a sheet of parchment paper, then fill it with dried rice, beans, or lentils.

Bake for 20 to 25 minutes, or until the edges of the dough have begun to brown. Remove the paper and rice, beans, or lentils (save them to use in this way again). Place the dough back in the oven for 4 to 5 additional minutes so that the bottom can dry out a bit, then remove from the oven and allow to cool. Remove from the mold when cool.

This method of baking a piecrust is called baking blind. The crust is baked through, permitting it to be filled with uncooked or precooked fillings at the last minute or with fillings that must be baked at a temperature too low to cook the crust.

Sweet Short Pastry Dough

LA PÂTE SABLÉE

INGREDIENTS FOR 1
POUND 1½ OUNCES
(500 g) DOUGH

1 egg yolk
2 tablespoons heavy cream
*1¼ sticks (150 g) butter, cut into
    8 pieces and allowed to soften*
1¾ cups (250 g) flour
½ teaspoon salt
*3 tablespoons (35 g) granulated
    sugar*
1 teaspoon baking powder

I t's best to make this dough the night before you want to use it.

Procedure

With a food processor: Place the egg yolk and cream in the bowl of the processor equipped with the metal blade. Run for 1 to 2 seconds to mix. Turn off the machine and add first the butter, then all the other ingredients in the order given. Run the machine for about 3 seconds, or until the mixture begins to stick together. Do *not* run long enough for it to form a ball. Dump the contents of the processor out onto a lightly floured table and pack into a ball, then place it in a plastic bag and chill for at least 1 hour or overnight.

By hand or with an electric mixer equipped with a dough hook: Beat the egg yolk and cream together until thick and foamy, then add all the other ingredients and beat with a wooden spoon or the dough hook until well mixed. Pack the dough into a ball, then place it in a plastic bag and chill for at least 1 hour or overnight.

Roll out and bake according to the directions given for Short Pastry Dough (p. 57).

Note: This dough is extremely soft and crumbly. It will probably break into pieces when you lift it to line the pie pan. Simply patch it and press the pieces together in the pan. Ed.

PREPARATION TIME

15 minutes, plus refrigeration time and 25 to 30 minutes to bake

Chocolate, Almond, and Orange Tart

TARTE DE CHOCOLAT, AUX AMANDES ET AUX ORANGES

This tart is made in advance but decorated at the last minute. It's best if you remove it from the refrigerator about 20 minutes before serving so that it won't be too cold.

Procedure

To make the piecrust: Place the chocolate and water in a small saucepan. Melt over low heat as described on page 29.

Stir the ground almonds and sugar together in a mixing bowl, then stir in the melted chocolate until a mixture of uniform color and texture is obtained.

Take a cake pan 8 inches (20 cm) wide and 1¼ inches (3 cm) high and line it with a sheet of aluminum foil. Press the foil well into the mold, with the edges of the foil extending out over the edges of the mold (see photo following p. 56).

Press the almond-chocolate mixture into the lined mold to a thickness of about ¼ inch (5 mm), covering the bottom and sides in the shape of a piecrust. Place in the freezer for 1 hour to harden.

To make the filling: Cut the orange zests into very thin (julienne) strips, then drop them into boiling water for 30 seconds; drain, cool under running water, and pat dry. Reserve.

Cut out 6 to 8 orange sections as described on page 71 and place in a tightly closed container in the refrigerator.

Place the chocolate and water in a small saucepan and melt over low heat as described on page 29. Remove from the heat and stir in the egg yolks, one at a time, then add the julienne of orange zests and the Cointreau.

INGREDIENTS FOR 6 SERVINGS

The Piecrust

2½ ounces (70 g) semisweet chocolate

2 tablespoons water

1 cup (125 g) ground almonds

5 tablespoons (60 g) granulated sugar

The Filling

Zest of 2 oranges

6 to 8 orange sections (1 orange)

5¼ ounces (150 g) semisweet chocolate

3 tablespoons (50 ml) water

3 egg yolks

1 tablespoon Cointreau

4 egg whites

1½ tablespoons (20 g) granulated sugar

PREPARATION TIME

The crust—20 to 25 minutes, plus 1 hour in the freezer; the filling—20 minutes, plus several hours to chill and set

In a mixing bowl, beat the egg whites until thick and foamy, add the sugar, and continue beating until very stiff. Fold in the chocolate mixture; the finished mixture should be of uniform color and texture.

Remove the piecrust from the freezer and fill it with the chocolate mixture. Place it in the refrigerator for several hours so that the filling can set.

To serve, lift the tart out of the mold by holding on to the edges of the aluminum foil. Fold down the foil on one side of the tart and begin sliding it onto a serving platter, folding the foil back underneath until the bottom of the tart is free, then peeling it off the other side.

Arrange the orange sections in a flower design in the center of the tart (see photo following p. 56) and serve.

Chocolate-Hazelnut-Coffee Tart

TARTE DE CHOCOLAT, AUX NOISETTES ET AU CAFÉ

INGREDIENTS FOR 6 TO 8 SERVINGS

⅔ cup (80 g) ground hazelnuts

½ cup (100 g) granulated sugar

4¼ ounces (125 g) semisweet chocolate

2 tablespoons milk

2 tablespoons (30 g) butter, broken into 3 pieces and allowed to soften

1½ pints (¾ l) coffee ice cream

2 cups (500 ml) Rum-Coffee Fudge Sauce (p. 122)

PREPARATION TIME

The piecrust—20 to 25 minutes; the sauce—15 to 20 minutes; plus freezing time

The crust can be made in advance and kept in the freezer, as can the chocolate sauce, which can be reheated in a double boiler.

Procedure

Line a cake pan 8 inches (20 cm) wide and 1¼ inches (3 cm) high with a sheet of aluminum foil, making sure that the foil is large enough that the edges extend well beyond the edges of the mold. Press the foil tightly against the mold.

Mix the hazelnuts and sugar together carefully so that a uniform mixture is formed.

Place the chocolate and milk in a saucepan and melt over low heat as described on page 29. Stir in the butter, piece by piece, then add the hazelnut-sugar mixture and stir together well.

Press the hazelnut paste into the lined mold in an even layer about ¼ inch (5 mm) thick, covering the bottom and sides of the mold like a piecrust. Place in the freezer to harden for at least 1 hour.

Remove the coffee ice cream from the freezer and place it in the refrigerator to soften for about 45 minutes; it should be soft enough to spread.

Spoon the ice cream into the hardened crust, smoothing the surface with a flexible-blade metal spatula. Now, lift the tart out of the mold by holding on to the aluminum foil extending out over the edge of the mold. Transfer it to a serving platter, peeling the foil down off one side first, then little by little easing the tart down onto the platter by folding the foil back and peeling it off the bottom and, finally, the remaining side.

Return the tart to the freezer until ready to serve. If the crust is filled several hours in advance, place the tart in the refrigerator for about 30 to 40 minutes before serving so that the ice cream won't be too hard.

To serve, make the Rum-Coffee Fudge sauce, or, if it was made in advance, reheat it. Pour a little in the center of the tart and spread it out to make a decorative circle (see photo following p. 56). Serve, with the rest of the sauce in a sauceboat.

Variations

1. Ground almonds may be used instead of ground hazelnuts to make the piecrust.

2. As in the picture following p. 56, a square mold may be used instead of a round one.

3. Instead of coffee ice cream the tart may be filled with any of the following: vanilla ice cream, Chocolate Ice Cream (p. 40), Chocolate or Kirsch-Flavored Pastry Cream (pp. 36, 37), or another filling of your choice.

Coconut-Chocolate Tart

TARTE À LA NOIX DE COCO ET AU CHOCOLAT

T he piecrust should be baked in advance. If desired, the entire tart may be made in advance and kept at room temperature.

Procedure

Make and bake a Sweet Short Pastry crust; leave it in the pan it was cooked in.

Preheat the oven to 350°F (175°C).

Place the water, sugar, and vanilla bean in a saucepan. Bring to a boil, add the coconut, stir, and allow to simmer for 20 minutes, stirring occasionally. The coconut should become transparent. Remove from the heat, lift out the vanilla bean, and stir in the rum and cinnamon. Allow to cool completely, then stir in the egg yolks, one by one.

In a mixing bowl, beat the egg whites until very stiff, then fold in the coconut mixture. Continue to fold until a uniform color and

INGREDIENTS FOR 6 TO 8 SERVINGS

1 baked piecrust made of Sweet Short Pastry Dough (p. 58)
1 cup (250 ml) water
1 cup (200 g) granulated sugar
½ vanilla bean, split in half lengthwise
1²/₃ cups (125 g) dried grated coconut
2 tablespoons light rum
½ teaspoon ground cinnamon
3 eggs, separated
½ recipe Simple Chocolate Icing (p. 115)

texture are obtained. Pour the mixture into the piecrust and bake for 40 minutes, or until the filling has risen somewhat and dried out on top. Remove from the oven and allow to cool.

To serve: Make the Simple Chocolate Icing and allow to cool to warm, then spread a thin coat of it over the surface of the coconut tart. Allow to cool to room temperature, turn out, and serve.

Chocolate-Walnut Tart

TARTE AU CHOCOLAT ET AUX NOIX

INGREDIENTS FOR 6
TO 8 SERVINGS

The Piecrust

2 1/4 cups (250 g) walnut meats
5 tablespoons (50 g) brown sugar
5 tablespoons (75 g) butter, cut
into pieces and allowed to
soften

The Filling

3/4 cup (200 ml) heavy
(whipping) cream
1/2 teaspoon instant coffee
3 tablespoons (50 ml) water
7 ounces (200 g) semisweet
chocolate
4 eggs
1 tablespoon dark rum
2 teaspoons vanilla sugar (see
note to Whipped Cream
with Melted Chocolate, p.
125)

PREPARATION TIME

The piecrust—20 to 25 minutes;
the filling—20 to 25 minutes;
plus freezing and refrigeration
time

T̄his tart is best made 1 to 2 days in advance.

Procedure

To make the piecrust: Place nutmeats in a food processor equipped with the metal blade and chop finely, pulsing rather than running the machine continuously. Add the brown sugar (make sure there are no hard lumps in it) and run the machine for a few seconds to mix the nuts and sugar together thoroughly. Add the butter and run the machine until the mixture begins to form a ball.

Line a cake pan 8 inches (20 cm) wide and 1 1/4 inches (3 cm) high with a sheet of aluminum foil, making sure that the foil is large enough that the edges extend well beyond the edges of the pan. Press the foil tightly into the corners of the mold.

Press the nut mixture into the lined pan, covering the bottom and sides with an even layer about 1/4 inch (5 mm) thick, like a piecrust. Place in the freezer for 1 hour to harden.

To make the filling: Place the cream in a mixing bowl and chill in the refrigerator.

Place the instant coffee and the water in a small saucepan. Stir to dissolve the coffee, then add the chocolate and melt over low heat as described on page 29. Keep warm.

In a mixing bowl, quickly beat the eggs and rum together, then beat in the melted chocolate.

Remove the cream from the refrigerator, add the vanilla sugar, and beat until it forms soft peaks. Carefully fold the whipped cream into the chocolate mixture until the mixture has a uniform color and texture.

Remove the hardened crust from the freezer and fill it with the chocolate mixture. Place in the refrigerator for at least 1 hour to set before serving.

To serve: Lift the tart out of the pan by holding on to the edges of the aluminum foil. Fold down the foil on one side of the tart and begin sliding it onto a serving platter, folding the foil back underneath until the bottom of the tart is free, then peeling it off the other side.

If you are not serving it immediately, return the tart to the refrigerator until ready to serve.

Variation

If desired, pecans may be used instead of walnuts in making the piecrust.

Monsieur Robert's Chocolate Tart with Pears

LA TARTE CHOCOLATÉE DE M. ROBERT À LA CRÈME ET AUX POIRES

M. Robert, a pastry chef from Quiberon, in Brittany, invented this tart. The dough is baked in a "Mary Anne pan," a special mold with a raised bottom. When the pastry base is turned out, there is an indentation in the top. The indentation is then filled, in this case with a chocolate pastry cream decorated with pears. By using different fillings, you can invent other tarts of your own.

Procedure

Preheat the oven to 350°F (175°C).

To make the pastry base: Sift the flour, cornstarch, and cocoa into a bowl, then stir in the ground almonds. Reserve.

Place the whole eggs, egg yolks, sugar, and honey in a medium saucepan over low heat and beat with an electric mixer set at medium speed for 5 to 10 minutes. The mixture should become very pale, foamy, and thick and greatly increase in volume. Test the temperature from time to time; if the mixture is too hot to dip your finger into and keep it there, remove the saucepan from the heat.

Fold in the dry ingredients reserved earlier, then the melted butter, to make a thick batter. Pour into a generously buttered 8½-

INGREDIENTS FOR 6 TO 8 SERVINGS

The Pastry Base

3 tablespoons (30 g) flour
1 tablespoon (10 g) cornstarch
1 tablespoon (10 g) unsweetened cocoa powder
1 tablespoon (10 g) ground almonds
2 whole eggs
2 egg yolks
3 tablespoons (40 g) granulated sugar
2 teaspoons (10 g) honey
2 teaspoons (10 g) butter, melted

The Filling

½ recipe Chocolate Pastry
    Cream (p. 36)
2 egg whites
4 to 6 poached or canned pear
    halves
Unsweetened cocoa powder

PREPARATION TIME

The pastry base—50 to 60
minutes; the filling—40 to 50
minutes

inch (22 cm) Mary Anne pan. Smooth the surface of the batter with a spoon or spatula. Bake for about 20 minutes, or until the dough begins to pull away from the sides of the pan.

Remove from the oven and immediately turn out onto a serving platter (see note). Allow to cool completely.

To make the filling: Make the Chocolate Pastry Cream, remove from the heat, and cover to keep hot.

Beat the egg whites until very stiff, then fold them into the hot pastry cream. Pour the mixture into a shallow dish so that it will cool off more quickly.

When the pastry cream is cool, spread it out into the indentation in the pastry base.

Drain the poached or canned pear halves and pat them dry in a clean cloth or dish towel. Cut each half lengthwise into 6 sections and arrange them in a flower pattern or in concentric circles on top of the pastry cream. Sprinkle very lightly with cocoa powder and serve.

Note: Because of its shape, doughs tend to stick to the bottom of the Mary Anne pan, especially when it is new. If using it for the first time, "prime" it by generously buttering it and placing it in the preheated oven for 10 minutes. Remove from the oven, allow to cool enough to handle, and wipe off any excess melted butter in it. Allow to cool completely, then generously butter once more, especially the flat, raised bottom surface. Pour in the batter and bake as described. Ed.

Chocolate-Caramel Quiche

QUICHE DE CHOCOLAT AU CARAMEL

The crust may be made and baked in advance, but the rest is done at the last minute.

Procedure

Make and bake the piecrust of your choice, but leave it in the pan it was cooked in.

Preheat the oven to 325°F (160°C).

To make the filling: Place the chocolate, water, and salt in a small saucepan and melt as described on page 29. Stir in the cinnamon, then allow to cool to warm.

In a mixing bowl, beat the egg yolks and cream together until of uniform color, then stir in the chocolate.

Pour the mixture into the piecrust, smooth the surface with a flexible-blade metal spatula, and bake for 30 to 35 minutes. The surface should look dry and cracked, and the filling should have risen considerably, but the center should be soft and creamy.

Remove the quiche from the oven and allow to cool about 30 minutes, until just warm (it's best that way).

To make the sauce: Place the sugar and water in a heavy-bottomed saucepan over moderate heat. Stir until the sugar has dissolved, add the lemon juice, then stop stirring and allow to cook until the sugar begins to change color. Swirl the saucepan to permit the sugar to color evenly; when it is a rich reddish gold, the caramel is ready.

Remove the caramel from the heat and allow it to cool for a few seconds until it has stopped bubbling. Add about ⅓ to ½ of the warm water (stand back, because it will splatter at first), then stir with a wooden spoon. When the water has dissolved most of the caramel, add the rest, stirring until the caramel has completely dissolved. Allow to cool to warm.

To serve, turn the warm quiche out onto a serving platter, spoon a little of the caramel sauce onto it, and spread it over the surface. Serve, with the rest of the sauce in a sauceboat.

Note: Although it's best to bake the quiche and make the sauce at the last minute, it is possible to make everything a few hours in advance and warm up the quiche in the oven and the sauce over very low heat just before serving. Ed.

INGREDIENTS FOR 6 SERVINGS

1 baked piecrust made of Short Pastry Dough (p. 57) or Sweet Short Pastry Dough (p. 58)

The Filling

9 ounces (250 g) semisweet chocolate
¼ cup (60 ml) water
1 pinch salt
½ teaspoon ground cinnamon
4 egg yolks
¾ cup (200 ml) crème fraîche (p. 30) or heavy cream

The Sauce

⅔ cup (125 g) granulated sugar
¼ cup water
5 to 6 drops lemon juice
¼ cup warm water

PREPARATION TIME

The piecrust—35 minutes; the filling—45 to 50 minutes; the sauce—10 minutes

PUFF PASTRIES

For the following desserts, you can either use frozen puff pastry (follow the instructions for using it that come on the package) or make it yourself. Although it is a rather tricky dough to make, and it takes a long time, it's well worth the effort.

Puff Pastry

LA PÂTE FEUILLETÉE

INGREDIENTS FOR 1
POUND 5 OUNCES
(600 g) DOUGH

*1¾ cups (250 g) flour, sifted
after measuring*

*3½ tablespoons (50 g) butter,
softened*

1 teaspoon (7 g) salt

½ cup (120 ml) cold water

*2¼ sticks (250 g) butter, kept
cold in the refrigerator*

PREPARATION TIME

*About 30 minutes, but variable
according to experience, plus
resting time*

Puff pastry is made in stages; it is very important to respect the resting periods in the refrigerator between "turns" (see below).

Procedure

Place the flour on the work surface and make a well in the center. Pour the water into the well and add the salt and softened butter. With your fingers, begin stirring the water and butter, pushing a little flour into the well as you do so with the other hand. When the mixture in the well has formed a thick paste, begin incorporating the rest of the flour with both hands, working with the tips of your fingers. Form the dough into a ball, flatten it slightly, and score the surface in a tic-tac-toe design with the tip of a knife. Place the dough in a plastic bag and allow to rest for 24 hours in the refrigerator.

To roll out: Remove the hard butter from the refrigerator and place it between 2 sheets of plastic wrap. Flatten it by hitting it with a rolling pin to form a square about 6 inches (15 cm) on a side.

Remove the dough from the refrigerator. Lightly flour the working surface and roll the dough out until it forms a square about 10 inches (25 cm) on a side.

Lay the butter on the dough so that the sides of the butter are facing the corners of the dough (kitty-corner). Fold 2 opposite corners of dough over the butter; they should overlap in the middle (if not, unfold, roll them out a bit longer with the rolling pin, then fold them again). Fold the remaining 2 corners over the butter. Make sure the dough overlaps so that no butter is visible. Press on the dough so that it sticks to itself.

Lightly flour the table, then roll out the dough into a long band about 16 inches long by 8 inches wide (40 × 20 cm). Always roll the rolling pin away from you, not back and forth. Fold the band in thirds to make a rectangle about 5¼ inches wide and 8 inches long (13 × 20 cm). You have just given the dough its first "turn."

Turn the dough ¼ turn to the right; the fold will now be running lengthwise away from you. Roll out and fold again exactly as described above. This is the second turn.

Place the dough in a plastic bag and chill in the refrigerator for 30 minutes. At the end of this time, remove it from the refrigerator and give it 2 more turns, as described above. Be careful! The dough will be more elastic and easier to work this time, so don't press too hard on the rolling pin, or the butter might break through (if it does, just pat flour on the broken place, chill the dough for a few minutes, and continue rolling). After giving the 2 turns, place the dough back in the plastic bag and chill for 30 minutes before giving it 2 last turns. When the dough has been given a total of 6 turns, it is ready to use.

Note: Making puff pastry is easiest in a cool room; in warm weather the butter melts so fast that it breaks through easily. It is extremely difficult, if not impossible, to make if the room temperature is above 80°F (27°C), although you might succeed if you chill a marble pastry board with ice trays while the dough is resting in the refrigerator.

On the other hand, puff pastry can be made, cut, and frozen for later use (it freezes very well). Ed.

To Cut and Bake Puff Pastry

PRÉPARATION ET CUISSON DES FEUILLETÉS

Procedure

Preheat the oven to 425°F (220°C).

After giving the sixth turn to the dough, roll it out on a lightly floured table into a rectangle about 15 by 10 inches (38 × 25 cm).

With a large, sharp knife, cut out 10 rectangles, each approximately 3 by 5 inches (8 × 12 cm). Do not pull the tip of the knife through the dough to cut, but push straight down on the blade with a slight rocking motion from the tip toward the handle. Trim off any uneven edges.

Place the rectangles on a baking sheet and brush them lightly with the beaten egg, making sure that the egg does not drip over the sides.

Bake for 5 minutes at 425°F (220°C), then lower the oven to 400°F (200°C) and bake for 15 to 20 minutes more, or until the

INGREDIENTS FOR 10 PUFF PASTRY RECTANGLES

1 pound 5 ounces (600 g) Puff Pastry dough (p. 66)
1 egg, lightly beaten

PREPARATION TIME

To roll out and cut—15 to 20 minutes; to bake—20 to 25 minutes

pastry is a rich golden brown. The rectangles are now ready to use, either hot or cold, depending on the recipe.

Note: If using puff pastry prepared in advance and frozen after cutting into rectangles, simply remove from the freezer, brush with egg, and place directly in the oven (do not thaw). Bake exactly as described. Ed.

Whipped-Cream Pastries with Caramel Custard Sauce

FEUILLETÉS DE CHANTILLY DE CHOCOLAT À LA CRÈME CARAMEL

INGREDIENTS FOR 6 SERVINGS

The Sauce

2 cups (½ l) milk
½ cup (100 g) granulated sugar
2 to 3 tablespoons water
5 egg yolks

The Pastries

6 puff pastry rectangles (see pp. 66–67)
Whipped Cream with Melted Chocolate (p. 125)

PREPARATION TIME

The pastry—35 to 45 minutes (to roll, cut, and bake after resting times); the whipped cream—15 minutes; the sauce —20 to 30 minutes

The pastries and sauce may be made in advance, and the cream may be whipped in advance, but the chocolate must be added to the whipped cream at the last minute. The dessert is assembled just before serving.

Procedure

To make the sauce: Place the milk in a saucepan and heat over low heat while making the caramel (if the milk boils, simply remove it from the heat).

In another saucepan, place the sugar and water and stir over moderate heat until the sugar has dissolved. Stop stirring and cook until the sugar begins to change color, then swirl the saucepan so that it will color evenly. When it is a rich, reddish gold color, remove from the heat, allow the bubbles to die down a bit, and add about ⅓ of the milk (stand back, it will splatter). Stir to dissolve the caramel a bit, then slowly add the rest of the milk, stirring until the caramel has completely dissolved.

Make a custard sauce exactly as described for Chocolate Custard Sauce (p. 123), substituting the caramel milk for the chocolate milk and using the number of egg yolks indicated here. Allow to cool, then reserve, covered, until ready to serve.

To assemble the pastries: Bake the pastry rectangles at the last minute, or bake them in advance and reheat.

Make the Whipped Cream with Melted Chocolate.

Remove the pastries from the oven, allow them to cool a bit, then cut them in half horizontally, forming a top and a bottom. Place a bottom in the center of each dessert plate, spoon the sauce around it, garnish with a large spoonful of the whipped cream, and cover with the pastry top. Serve immediately.

Chocolate Pastries with Coffee Custard Sauce

FEUILLETÉS DE CHOCOLAT À LA CRÈME AU CAFÉ

Each element of this dessert can be made in advance, then assembled at the last minute.

Procedure

Make the Whipped-Cream Chocolate Mousse and reserve in the refrigerator.

Make the Coffee Custard Sauce, allow to cool, and reserve, covered, at room temperature.

Grate the chocolate and reserve in the refrigerator.

To serve, either bake the pastry rectangles at the last minute or bake them in advance and reheat. Remove from the oven, allow to cool slightly, then cut each one in half horizontally, forming a top and a bottom. Place the bottoms on individual dessert plates and garnish with a large spoonful of chocolate mousse, rounded in a dome.

Set the top of each pastry at an angle over the mousse, so that the mousse can be seen inside. Spoon a nice amount of coffee sauce around each pastry, sprinkle the grated chocolate over the sauce, and serve immediately.

INGREDIENTS FOR 6 SERVINGS

Whipped-Cream Chocolate Mousse (p. 33)
Coffee Custard Sauce (p. 124)
3½ ounces (100 g) semisweet chocolate
6 puff pastry rectangles (see pp. 66–67)

PREPARATION TIME

The pastry—35 to 45 minutes (to roll, cut, and bake after resting times); the mousse—30 to 35 minutes; the sauce—15 to 20 minutes

Kirsch-Flavored Pastries with Two Sauces

FEUILLETÉS DE CRÈME AU KIRSCH AUX DEUX SAUCES

Everything may be made in advance and assembled just before serving.

Procedure

Make the Kirsch-Flavored Pastry Cream and the Chocolate Custard Sauce and reserve in the refrigerator.

Bake the pastry rectangles, or bake them in advance and reheat. Make the Hot Fudge Sauce, or make in advance and reheat in a double boiler.

Remove the pastries from the oven, allow to cool slightly, then cut in half horizontally to make a top and a bottom. Place a bottom

INGREDIENTS FOR 6 SERVINGS

Kirsch-Flavored Pastry Cream (p. 37)
Chocolate Custard Sauce (p. 123)
6 puff pastry rectangles (see pp. 66–67)
½ recipe Hot Fudge Sauce (p. 123)

PREPARATION TIME

The pastry—35 to 45 minutes (to roll, cut, and bake after resting times); the pastry cream —20 to 25 minutes; the custard sauce—15 to 20 minutes; the fudge sauce—30 to 35 minutes

on each dessert plate and garnish with a large spoonful of the pastry cream. Set the top in place.

Spoon the custard sauce around the pastries. Then, using a teaspoon, drop large drops of Hot Fudge Sauce here and there into it. When the hot sauce hits the cold sauce, it will immediately stiffen. Serve immediately.

Frangipane Pastries with Pears and Chocolate Sauce

FEUILLETÉS DE FRANGIPANE AUX POIRES, À LA SAUCE AU CHOCOLAT

INGREDIENTS FOR 6 SERVINGS

6 puff pastry rectangles (see pp. 66–67)
Hot Chocolate Sauce (p. 120)
6 poached or canned pear halves

The Frangipane

6 tablespoons (60 g) confectioners' sugar
Scant ⅔ cup (75 g) ground almonds
5 tablespoons (75 g) butter, softened
1 whole egg
1 teaspoon dark rum.

PREPARATION TIME

The pastry—35 to 45 minutes, (to roll, cut, and bake after resting times); the sauce—15 minutes; the frangipane—10 minutes

The pastry rectangles and sauce may be made in advance, but the frangipane should be made as close as possible to serving time. The dessert is assembled at the last minute.

Procedure

Bake the pastry rectangles, or bake them in advance and reheat.

Make the Hot Chocolate Sauce and allow to cool to warm, or make in advance and reheat to warm, stirring over low heat.

Drain the pears and pat them dry in a clean cloth or dish towel. Cut them crosswise into thin slices. Leave each half together.

To make the frangipane: In a bowl, mix the sugar and ground almonds.

In a separate bowl, beat the butter with a fork or wooden spoon until it is the consistency of a thick cream. Sprinkle the sugar-almond mixture over the butter, and beat vigorously with the spoon to incorporate air and make the mixture light. Stir in the egg and finally the rum. Reserve at room temperature.

Remove the pastries from the oven and allow to cool to warm. Preheat the broiler.

Cut the pastries in half horizontally to form a top and a bottom. Carefully place a sliced half pear on each bottom, pushing lightly from the narrow end of the pear toward the wide end to make the slices "lie down" and overlap slightly. Generously spread each pear with frangipane, then place the pastries on a baking sheet and brown the frangipane under the broiler (this takes only a few seconds).

Remove from the broiler, place a pastry in the center of each dessert plate, set the top in place, and spoon the warm chocolate sauce around each one. Serve immediately.

Pastries with Chocolate Mousse and Oranges

FEUILLETÉS DE MOUSSE DE CHOCOLAT AUX ORANGES

Although everything may be prepared in advance, the dessert should be assembled just before serving.

Procedure

Make the Chocolate Mousse with Candied Orange Peel well in advance so that it will have time to chill and set.

To prepare the orange sections: Cut off both ends of each orange, then set it on end and cut off all of the peel, exposing the orange flesh. Run the tip of the knife between each orange section and the membranes on either side of it. Place the peeled sections in a container that can be tightly closed; save any juice in the bowl and use it along with the juice of the other 4 oranges. Cover the container and place it in the refrigerator until ready to serve.

Strain the orange juice, then sweeten it according to your taste with the sugar syrup (see note). Reserve in the refrigerator.

Bake the pastry rectangles, or bake in advance and reheat. Remove from the oven and cut in half horizontally to form a top and a bottom.

Arrange 6 orange sections in a semicircle along the edge of half of each dessert plate, then place a pastry bottom at the opposite edge and garnish with a large spoonful of mousse (see photo following p. 72). Spoon a little sauce between the orange sections to cover the bottom of the plate, set the pastry top in place, and serve immediately.

Comment: The mousse will melt slightly when it comes in contact with the hot pastry—this makes it absolutely delicious. But you must work very quickly to avoid its melting completely and to avoid having the sauce make the pastry base soggy.

Note: Either use commercial cane sugar syrup or make your own: To every 3 tablespoons water add 4 tablespoons sugar. Bring to a rolling boil, remove from the heat, and allow to cool. Ed.

INGREDIENTS FOR 6 SERVINGS

Chocolate Mousse with Candied Orange Peel (p. 33)
4 to 6 oranges (to make a total of 36 orange sections)
Juice of 4 oranges
Sugar syrup (see note)
6 puff pastry rectangles (see pp. 66–67)

PREPARATION TIME

The mousse—25 minutes; the orange sections—15 minutes; the sauce—5 to 10 minutes; the pastry—35 to 45 minutes (to roll, cut, and bake after resting times)

PROFITEROLES

Profiteroles are miniature cream puff pastries filled with a sherbet or ice cream and served with a sauce. The pastries themselves are very easy to make, and they keep for up to a week in a plastic bag in the refrigerator.

Here's how to make them.

Cream Puff Pastry

LA PÂTE À CHOUX

INGREDIENTS FOR
ABOUT 30 CREAM
PUFFS

½ cup (120 ml) water, mixed with ½ cup (120 ml) milk
7 tablespoons (110 g) butter
1 teaspoon salt
1 teaspoon granulated sugar
1 cup (140 g) flour, sifted after measuring
5 whole eggs

PREPARATION TIME

45 minutes

Procedure

Preheat the oven to 425°F (220°C).

Place the milk-water mixture along with the butter, salt, and sugar in a saucepan and bring to a boil.

As soon as the mixture is boiling and the butter has completely melted, remove from the heat and add all the flour at once, stirring. Return to the heat and cook for about 1 minute, stirring vigorously, until the ball of dough detaches completely from the sides of the pan.

Remove from the heat, allow to cool for a few minutes, then stir in the eggs, one at a time. Beat the dough with a wooden spoon until very smooth.

Spoon the dough into a pastry bag equipped with a ⅝-inch (15 mm) nozzle (a pastry bag is essential if you want nice, round cream puffs). Butter and flour a baking sheet, then squeeze out little mounds of batter about 1¼ inches (3 cm) wide, leaving a good inch (2.5 cm) between them.

Bake for 15 minutes, then set the oven door slightly ajar by inserting the handle of a wooden spoon. Cook 15 minutes more, or until the cream puffs look dry and are a nice golden brown color.

Remove from the oven and allow to cool before using.

Puff Pastry with Chocolate Mousse and Oranges (page 71)

Vanilla Profiteroles with Hot Chocolate Sauce (page 73)

Pineapple Belle-Hélène and Sponge Cake with Chocolate-Covered
Strawberries (pages 84, 85)

Summer Fondue (page 86)

Chocolate Profiteroles with Vanilla Sauce

PROFITEROLES DE GLACE AU CHOCOLAT
À LA CRÈME À LA VANILLE

Everything is made in advance and assembled just before serving.

Procedure

Make the Chocolate Ice Cream at least a day in advance and keep in the freezer.

Make the Custard Sauce and keep in the refrigerator.

Make the cream puff pastries and keep sealed in the refrigerator.

About 45 minutes before serving, transfer the ice cream from the freezer to the refrigerator to soften and remove the sauce from the refrigerator so that it will be at room temperature when served.

Cut a horizontal slit in each cream puff pastry and fill it with a scoop of ice cream. Place 3 profiteroles on each plate, pour a little of the sauce over each one, then pour enough sauce onto the bottom of the plate to cover it. Serve immediately.

INGREDIENTS FOR 4
SERVINGS

1 pint (½ l) Chocolate Ice Cream (p. 40)
1⅔ cups (375 ml) Vanilla Custard Sauce (p. 124)
12 cream puff pastries (p. 72)

PREPARATION TIME

The pastries—45 minutes; the sauce—20 minutes; the ice cream—20 to 25 minutes

Vanilla Profiteroles with Hot Chocolate Sauce

PROFITEROLES DE GLACE À LA VANILLE, SAUCE CHOCOLAT

Everything can be made in advance and assembled just before serving.

Procedure

About 45 minutes before serving, transfer the ice cream to the refrigerator so that it will have time to soften.

Make the Hot Chocolate Sauce and keep it at room temperature; just before serving, reheat in a double boiler.

Cut a horizontal slit in each cream puff to open it and fill it with a scoop of ice cream (see photo following p. 72). Place 3 profiteroles on each dessert plate, pour a little of the sauce over each one, then pour enough sauce onto the bottom of the plate to cover it completely. Serve immediately.

INGREDIENTS FOR 4
SERVINGS

1 pint (½ l) vanilla ice cream
1⅔ cups (375 ml) Hot Chocolate Sauce (p. 120)
12 cream puff pastries (p. 72)

PREPARATION TIME

The pastries—45 minutes; the sauce—10 minutes

Hazelnut Profiteroles with Hot Fudge Sauce

PROFITEROLES DE GLACE À LA NOISETTE ET À LA HOT FUDGE SAUCE

INGREDIENTS FOR 4 SERVINGS

1 pint (½ l) hazelnut ice cream
Hot Fudge Sauce (p. 123)
12 cream puff pastries (p. 72)
About ¼ cup (40 g) chopped hazelnuts

PREPARATION TIME

The pastries—45 minutes; the sauce—25 minutes

E verything can be made in advance and assembled just before serving.

Procedure

About 45 minutes before serving, transfer the ice cream from the freezer to the refrigerator so that it will have time to soften.

Make the Hot Fudge Sauce and keep at room temperature. Just before serving, reheat over low heat, stirring.

Cut off the tops of the cream puff pastries about ⅔ of the way up. Fill each with a scoop of ice cream that sticks up a bit (discard the tops of the pastries).

Place 3 profiteroles on each dessert plate. Pour a little of the sauce over each one, then pour enough sauce onto the bottom of each plate to cover it completely. Sprinkle each profiterole with chopped hazelnuts and serve immediately.

Pistachio Profiteroles with Honey-Flavored Chocolate Sauce

PROFITEROLES DE GLACE À LA PISTACHE À LA SAUCE CHOCOLAT AU MIEL

INGREDIENTS FOR 4 SERVINGS

1⅔ cups (375 ml) Honey-Flavored Chocolate Sauce (p. 121)
Grated chocolate for decoration
1 pint (½ l) pistachio ice cream
12 cream puff pastries (p. 72)

PREPARATION TIME

The pastries—45 minutes; the sauce—10 to 12 minutes

E verything can be made in advance and assembled at the last minute.

Procedure

Make the Honey-Flavored Chocolate Sauce and reserve it in the refrigerator.

Grate the chocolate and keep it in a covered bowl in the refrigerator.

About 45 minutes before serving, transfer the ice cream from the freezer to the refrigerator so that it will have time to soften.

Cut off the tops of the cream puff pastries about ⅔ of the way up (discard the tops). Fill each pastry with a scoop of ice cream that sticks up a bit. Place 3 profiteroles on each dessert plate and pour enough sauce around them to cover the bottom of the plate. Sprinkle the ice cream with a little grated chocolate and serve immediately.

Passion Fruit Profiteroles with Bananas and Chocolate Sauce

PROFITEROLES EXOTIQUES AU CHOCOLAT

E verything but the bananas can be prepared in advance. The dessert is assembled just before serving.

Procedure

Make the Chocolate Custard Sauce and reserve it in the refrigerator.

About 30 minutes before serving, transfer the sherbet from the freezer to the refrigerator so that it will have time to soften.

Cut the tops of the cream puff pastries off about ⅔ of the way up (discard the tops). Place 3 pastries on each dessert plate.

Peel the bananas and cut off each end, then cut them into very thick, ¾-inch (2 cm) slices. In a large frying pan, melt the butter over moderate heat until it no longer sizzles. Lay the bananas in the pan so that they are all touching the bottom, lower the heat, and allow to cook for about 5 minutes. With a spatula, carefully turn them over and cook for about 5 minutes on the other side.

While the bananas are cooking, fill each cream puff pastry with a scoop of sherbet, allowing it to stick up a bit. Pour enough sauce around the profiteroles to cover the bottom of the plates.

With a small, flexible-blade spatula, remove the banana slices one at a time and place them in the sauce at the edge of each plate, forming a circle around the profiteroles. Serve immediately.

INGREDIENTS FOR 4 SERVINGS

½ recipe Chocolate Custard Sauce (p. 123)
1 pint (½ l) passion fruit sherbet
12 cream puff pastries (p. 72)
3 bananas, not quite ripe
5 tablespoons (75 g) butter

PREPARATION TIME

The pastries—45 minutes; the sauce—10 to 15 minutes; the bananas—15 minutes

3

Fondues
Sweet Omelets
Puddings
and Various Other
Desserts

Sponge Cake with Chocolate-Covered Strawberries (Croûtes de fraises glacées de chocolat), p. 85

Summer Fondue (Fondue d'été), p. 86

Winter Fondue (Fondue d'hiver), p. 87

Chocolate Omelet with Vanilla Ice Cream (Omelette au chocolat, glace à la vanille), p. 88

Rum Omelet with Rum-Coffee Fudge Sauce (Omelette au rhum, fudge de chocolat, rhum et café), p. 89

Snow Eggs with Chocolate-Caramel Custard Sauce (Oeufs à la neige, crème au chocolat caramélisé), p. 90

Chocolate Pudding (Petits pots de crème), p. 91

Spice Pudding (Pudding aux épices), p. 91

Date-Nut Pudding (Pudding aux dattes et aux amandes), p. 93

Steamed Chocolate-Nut Pudding (Pudding à l'étouffé de noix et de café), p. 93

Puff Pastry Orange Fritters with Orange-Flavored Chocolate Sauce (Rissoles d'oranges à la sauce chocolat à l'orange), p. 94

Chocolate "Soup" with French-Toast "Croutons" (Soupe de chocolat au pain perdu), p. 95

Chocolate Soufflé (Soufflé au chocolat), p. 96

This chapter contains various desserts, many of which are hard to classify. Some of them can be prepared in advance, others must be made at the last minute, still others in several steps. Any one of them is the perfect end to either a simple family dinner or a more formal one.

Here you will find some classic French desserts, some of my own inventions, and even some American desserts. None of them is really difficult; you simply need to be a little organized.

Pear Custard with Chocolate Sauce

FLAN DE POIRES AU CHOCOLAT

The custard is made in advance and chilled, but the sauce is made just before serving.

Procedure

Peel the pears and cut each one into 6 to 8 wedges, depending on their size. Melt the butter in a large frying pan or *sauteuse,* and brown the pears on all sides over moderate heat. Sprinkle with the flour and stir gently for about 1 minute to allow the flour to cook a bit, then stir in the water and sugar and add the vanilla bean. Allow to simmer until the pears are perfectly tender, then lift them out of the cooking liquid with a skimmer or slotted spoon and place them in a serving dish. Reserve the cooking liquid in the pan.

In a bowl, beat the egg yolks lightly with 1 tablespoon of the cooking liquid. Stir in 2 more tablespoons of the liquid, then pour the egg mixture into the pan along with the rest of the liquid. Cook, stirring constantly, over low heat until the mixture becomes the consistency of a nice thick sauce. *Do not allow to boil.* Remove from the heat, lift out the vanilla bean, pour over the pears, and stir gently to distribute the pears evenly. Place in the refrigerator to chill before serving.

About 20 minutes before serving, remove the dessert from the refrigerator so that it won't be too cold. Sprinkle with a little cocoa powder. Make the Hot Chocolate Sauce and keep warm over very low heat (the sauce may be made at the last minute if preferred). Serve the custard in the serving dish and the sauce in a sauceboat.

Comment: The custard may be served hot instead of cold. In this case, brown the surface of the warm custard under the broiler and serve with a cold Chocolate Custard Sauce (p. 123).

INGREDIENTS FOR 6 SERVINGS

*6 to 8 pears (depending on size),
  not too ripe
3 tablespoons (45 g) butter
1 tablespoon (10 g) flour
½ cup (120 ml) water
⅓ cup (75 g) granulated sugar
1 vanilla bean, split in half
  lengthwise
2 egg yolks
Unsweetened cocoa powder
1⅔ cups (375 ml) Hot Chocolate
  Sauce (p. 120)*

PREPARATION TIME

The pears—10 minutes; the custard—15 to 20 minutes; the sauce—7 to 8 minutes

Banana Fritters with Creamy Fudge Sauce

BANANES FRITES, HOT FUDGE À LA CRÈME

INGREDIENTS FOR 8 SERVINGS

The Batter

½ teaspoon granulated dry yeast
1 tablespoon milk, warmed
Scant 1 cup (120 g) flour
1 egg, separated
¼ teaspoon salt
6 tablespoons (100 ml) milk
3 tablespoons (50 ml) beer
1 tablespoon oil

The Bananas

3 large bananas
Juice of 1 lemon
2 tablespoons granulated sugar
1 tablespoon dark rum (more or less, to taste)

Hot Fudge Sauce (p. 123)
6 tablespoons (100 ml) crème fraîche (p. 30) or heavy cream
Deep-frying oil
Granulated sugar

PREPARATION TIME

The batter—20 minutes; the bananas—10 minutes; the sauce—20 minutes; the fritters —about 3 minutes per batch

T he bananas are flavored in advance and fried just before serving.

Procedure

To make the fritter batter: Two hours before frying, dissolve the yeast in a small bowl with the warm milk.

Place the flour in a mixing bowl and make a well in the center. Place the egg yolk, yeast mixture, and salt in the well. Stir to break up the egg yolk and mix it with the yeast, then add 2 tablespoons of the milk and all of the beer to the well. Stir, incorporating the flour little by little, and adding a little more milk until a mixture like a thick cake batter is formed. Beat vigorously with a spoon to eliminate all lumps, then add the oil and the rest of the milk, stirring. The finished mixture should be relatively liquid. Cover with a dish towel and allow to rest at room temperature until ready to use. Just before frying, beat the egg white until very stiff and fold into the batter.

To prepare the bananas: One hour before frying, peel the bananas and remove the "strings," then cut off the ends and cut into thick, ⅝- to ¾-inch (1.5 to 2 cm) slices. Place in a mixing bowl, pour over the lemon juice, sprinkle with the sugar, and add the rum. Mix together well with your fingers to avoid breaking the bananas, and reserve at room temperature.

Make the Hot Fudge Sauce and allow to cool, then add the cream, stirring vigorously to obtain a creamy consistency, not too thick.

Just before frying, remove the banana slices from the bowl and dry them on paper towels.

Preheat the oven to warm and heat the oil in a deep fryer. Spread out some paper towels to drain the fritters on, and get a plateful of granulated sugar ready to roll the fritters in.

Heat the oil to 350°F (175°C); if you don't have a deep-frying or sugar thermometer, drop a little of the batter into the oil—when hot enough, the batter should bounce immediately to the surface of the oil and begin to sizzle.

One at a time, dip the slices of banana into the batter and drop them into the hot oil. Place as many of them in the fryer as you can without crowding them. When they are a pale gold color on the first side, turn them over to cook the other side, then lift them out with a skimmer or slotted spoon and drain on the paper towels. Start the second batch of fritters going, then roll the first batch in the sugar and place on a platter in the oven to keep warm. (Each batch should take no more than 3 minutes to cook if the oil is hot enough.) Cook as many batches as necessary.

Either serve on the serving platter with the sauce in a sauceboat, or serve 4 to 5 fritters on each individual dessert plate with some sauce poured around them.

Chocolate Blinis with Pears and Chocolate Sabayon

BLINIS DE CHOCOLAT, POIRES FONDUES, SABAYON DE CHOCOLAT

The batter is made 2 to 3 hours before cooking. The pears may be cooked in advance, then reheated over low heat, stirring gently. The sabayon sauce is made at the last minute, as are the blinis.

Procedure

To make the blinis: Dissolve the yeast in about 1 tablespoon of the milk, then add the rest.

Sift the flour, cocoa, and sugar together into a mixing bowl. Add the salt, then stir in the egg yolks and the melted butter. Little by little, stir in the yeast-milk mixture; when the batter has reached the consistency of a thick cake batter, beat it vigorously with a spoon to eliminate any lumps. Continue stirring in the milk little by little—the finished batter should be quite liquid.

Place the batter in a warm place and cover with a dish towel. Allow to rest for 2 to 3 hours.

When ready to make the blinis, preheat the oven to warm. Remove the egg white from the refrigerator and beat until stiff. Stir the batter, then fold in the egg white.

To cook the blinis, use a special little frying pan called a blini pan (see note). Grease it lightly with a little butter, add 2 tablespoons batter, and cook for about 1 minute over low heat. With a spatula, turn the blini over and cook for 1 minute on the second side, then place on a serving platter and keep warm while cooking the other blinis (the finished blinis should be quite thick and light).

INGREDIENTS FOR 8 SERVINGS

The Blinis

½ teaspoon granulated dry yeast
1 cup (¼ l) milk, warmed
¾ cup (100 g) flour
2 tablespoons (20 g) unsweetened cocoa powder
¼ cup (50 g) granulated sugar
1 pinch salt
2 egg yolks
2 tablespoons (30 g) butter, melted
1 egg white, kept in the refrigerator

The Pears

6 to 7 medium pears
2 tablespoons (30 g) butter
1 tablespoon granulated sugar

Chocolate Sabayon (p. 122)
Unsweetened cocoa powder

FONDUES, OMELETS, PUDDINGS

PREPARATION TIME

The batter—20 minutes, plus resting time; the blinis—(to cook) about 2 minutes each; the pears—about 10 minutes; the Chocolate Sabayon—15 to 20 minutes

To prepare the pears: Peel the pears, core them, and cut them lengthwise into thin slices.

Melt the butter in a frying pan, add the pears, sprinkle with the sugar, and allow to cook over low heat, covered, until there is no liquid left and the pears are soft, shiny, and somewhat transparent. Set aside away from the heat.

Make the Chocolate Sabayon and remove from the heat.

To serve: Place a blini in the center of each dessert plate and arrange a little pile of pears on top of each one. Surround the blinis with the sauce, sprinkle the pears with a tiny bit of cocoa powder to make them look pretty, and serve immediately.

Note: It is best to have several blini pans so that more than one can be cooked at a time. Otherwise, cook 4 blinis at a time in a large frying pan (use 2 tablespoons of batter for each one). Since they will spread out a bit more than those done in a blini pan, they may take less time to cook, so make sure they don't burn. Ed.

Brioche with Almond Cream and Chocolate Custard Sauce

BRIOCHES À LA CRÈME D'AMANDES ET AU CHOCOLAT

INGREDIENTS FOR 6 SERVINGS

4 tablespoons (60 g) butter, softened
½ cup (75 g) confectioners' sugar
½ cup (75 g) ground almonds
1 egg, lightly beaten
1 tablespoon (10 g) cornstarch
1 teaspoon kirsch
1 cylindrical brioche (brioche mousseline) (see note)
2 cups (½ l) Chocolate Custard Sauce (p. 123)

PREPARATION TIME

The almond cream—15 to 20 minutes; the sauce—15 to 20 minutes

 he sauce may be made in advance, but everything else must be done just before serving.

Procedure

In a mixing bowl, beat the butter with a fork until it is the consistency of a smooth, thick cream.

In a second bowl, mix the confectioners' sugar and ground almonds together, then add this, little by little, to the creamed butter, still beating with a fork. When smooth and light, add the beaten egg. When smooth, beat in the cornstarch and the kirsch. The finished mixture should be very smooth and creamy.

Preheat the oven to 525°F (275°C) and place a baking sheet inside to heat up.

Cut the brioche into 6 thick slices (about 1 inch [2.5 cm] each). Spread them with a thick layer of almond cream, then place in the hot oven for 5 to 6 minutes to brown lightly.

Place on a serving platter and serve, with a sauceboat of Chocolate Custard Sauce on the side.

Note: If brioche is unavailable, egg bread may be used. In this case, rather than cutting straight down, lean the knife at a slant—this will make the slices taller. Ed.

Crêpes with Chocolate Filling

CRÊPES AU CHOCOLAT

T he crêpes may be made in advance and reheated by being piled up on a plate, covered with aluminum foil, and placed over a pot of boiling water. Nevertheless, they are better if prepared just before serving and kept warm in the oven with the door ajar. The sauce can be made in advance.

Procedure

About 1 to 2 hours before you plan to make the crêpes, make the batter by placing the flour, salt, and eggs in a mixing bowl and stirring to mix coarsely. Add enough milk to make a mixture the consistency of a thick cake batter, then beat with a wooden spoon to remove any lumps. Continue adding the milk little by little, using a whisk rather than a spoon when the batter begins to thin out; when ready, it should be about the consistency of heavy cream. Whisk in the oil and rum (if using) and allow to sit for 1 to 2 hours.

Preheat the oven to 300°F (150°C). Place a crêpe pan, 6 inches (15 cm) in diameter, over moderate heat and grease with a small lump of butter. Stir the batter, then, when the pan is very hot, pour the equivalent of about 2½ tablespoons (40 ml) batter in it, tipping and turning the pan so that the batter will cover the bottom (all the batter must be placed in the pan at once, so measure it into a small bowl, or use a large spoon that holds the correct amount). Cook the crêpe for about 1 minute on the first side, then turn it over and cook for 1 minute on the other side. Place on a plate in the preheated oven with the door ajar to keep warm while making the other crêpes: there should be 12 crêpes in all.

Make the Hot Fudge Sauce and allow to cool until very thick.

Preheat the broiler.

Set out a heatproof platter large enough to hold the 12 crêpes folded in half and overlapping slightly.

One at time, spread a good spoonful of fudge sauce over ½ of each crêpe, fold the other half over it, and place on the platter. When all the crêpes are on the platter, sprinkle with confectioners' sugar and place under the broiler for a few seconds to caramelize. Serve immediately.

INGREDIENTS FOR 6 SERVINGS (12 SMALL CRÊPES)

1¾ cups (250 g) flour
½ teaspoon salt
4 whole eggs
2 cups (½ l) milk
2 tablespoons cooking oil
2 tablespoons dark rum (optional)
Butter
Hot Fudge Sauce (p. 123)
Confectioners' sugar

PREPARATION TIME

The batter—10 minutes plus resting time; the crêpes—(to cook) 24 minutes; the sauce—25 minutes

Pineapple Belle-Hélène

ANANAS BELLE-HÉLÈNE

INGREDIENTS FOR 6 SERVINGS

1½ pints (¾ l) vanilla ice cream
Hot Chocolate Sauce (p. 120)
6 slices canned pineapple

PREPARATION TIME

The sauce—10 minutes; the dessert—15 to 20 minutes

T his super-quick dessert is made just before serving.

Procedure

About 40 minutes before serving, transfer the ice cream from the freezer to the refrigerator in order to soften.

Make the Hot Chocolate Sauce; keep warm over very low heat.

Cut each pineapple slice into 6 pieces. Take 6 pretty dessert dishes and arrange 6 pieces of pineapple around the edge of each one, then place a large scoop of ice cream in the middle. Pour the Hot Chocolate Sauce over the ice cream and serve immediately.

Variation

Traditionally, this dessert is made with poached pears. In this case, place the ice cream in the dish, the pear on top to one side, and pour the chocolate sauce over.

Cocoa-Hazelnut Cream

CRÈME DE CACAO AUX NOISETTES

INGREDIENTS FOR 6 SERVINGS

1 tablespoon cornstarch
6 tablespoons (60 g) ground hazelnuts
¾ cup (100 g) unsweetened cocoa powder
⅔ cup (125 g) granulated sugar
1 pinch salt
1½ cups (350 ml) milk
3 egg yolks
1 tablespoon dark rum
3 tablespoons (45 g) butter, cut into 4 pieces and allowed to soften
6 slices brioche or egg bread

PREPARATION TIME

15 to 20 minutes

T his dessert is made in advance and served with slices of brioche, toasted just before serving.

Procedure

In a mixing bowl, combine the cornstarch, ground hazelnuts, cocoa, sugar, and salt.

In a saucepan away from the heat, whisk the milk into the egg yolks, then stir enough of this mixture into the dry mixture to form a very thick batter. Beat with a spoon to remove any lumps, then stir in the rest of the milk mixture little by little.

Pour everything back into the saucepan and place over moderate heat. Bring to a boil, stirring constantly, then allow to boil gently for 2 to 3 minutes, still stirring. Remove from the heat, add the rum, then stir in the butter, a piece at a time.

Pour the cream into a serving dish and cover with plastic wrap. Allow to cool, then chill until ready to serve. Serve accompanied with slices of brioche or egg bread, lightly toasted at the last minute.

Sponge Cake with Chocolate-Covered Strawberries

CROÛTES DE FRAISES GLACÉES DE CHOCOLAT

The dessert may be made in advance and kept in the refrigerator, and the icing should be spooned over the strawberries about 30 minutes before serving.

Procedure

Make the Chocolate Sponge Cake; set aside.

In a saucepan, mix the cream, ⅔ of the milk, the sugar, and the vanilla bean. Bring barely to a boil, stirring constantly, then remove from the heat.

Beat the egg yolks lightly with the remaining milk, then pour the hot milk over them, whisking constantly. Pour back into the saucepan and place over low heat, stirring constantly until thick enough to lightly coat a spoon (if you draw a horizontal line in the sauce on the spoon, it should hold its shape). *Do not allow it to boil*, or the sauce will curdle. Remove from the heat, stir in the kirsch, then strain into a mixing bowl. Allow to cool, whisking from time to time, then place in the refrigerator for at least 2 hours to chill and thicken before using.

Wash the strawberries, pat them dry in paper towels, then remove the stems and set aside at room temperature.

Cut 6 slices of the sponge cake, each about ⅝ inch (1.5 cm) thick. Arrange them on a serving platter and brush them generously with the water-kirsch mixture. The cake should be quite moist. Allow to sit while the cream is chilling.

When the cream is ready, spread a thick layer in the center of each slice of cake (see photo following p. 72). Arrange 3 nice strawberries on the cream.

About 1 hour before serving, make the icing; allow it to cool to lukewarm and thicken a bit, then spoon a little onto each strawberry.

Allow the icing to cool to room temperature and set, then serve.

INGREDIENTS FOR 6 SERVINGS

Chocolate Sponge Cake (p. 56)
¾ cup (200 ml) heavy cream
¾ cup (200 ml) milk
½ cup (100 g) granulated sugar
1 vanilla bean, split in half lengthwise
5 egg yolks
1 tablespoon kirsch
18 large strawberries—purchase ¾ pound (350 g)
3 tablespoons (50 ml) water, mixed with 3 tablespoons (50 ml) kirsch
¼ recipe Simple Chocolate Icing (p. 115)

PREPARATION TIME

The Chocolate Sponge Cake— 40 to 50 minutes; the cream—20 to 25 minutes; assembling the dessert—15 to 20 minutes; the icing—10 minutes

FONDUES

Fondues should be served only to real chocolate lovers, and only after an extremely light meal.

The idea is simple: in the middle of the table is a chafing dish full of hot chocolate sauce. Each person has a plate, wooden skewers, a long-handled fondue fork, and a spoon.

Placed on either side or around the chafing dish, on the table, are plates or bowls full of the ingredients that will be dipped into the chocolate sauce with the help of the skewers or fork, and little bowls of sugar, cocoa powder, and the like that each delicious mouthful can be rolled in, to give it another note of flavor.

There should be plenty of each element, but the choice should be carefully made. Generally, it is best to have some fresh, light ingredients such as fruits, others dry and crunchy.

Following are two suggestions.

Summer Fondue

FONDUE D'ÉTÉ

INGREDIENTS FOR 8
SERVINGS

The Fruits

½ pound (250 g) strawberries, washed, drained, and stemmed
½ pound (250 g) cherries, washed and pitted
½ pound (250 g) raspberries
4 to 5 pears, peeled, cored, and cut into cubes, mixed with the juice of 1 lemon (to prevent discoloration)

The Crunchy Elements

4 to 5 slices toast, buttered
8 lady fingers
8 vanilla wafers
8 small puff pastry cookies (palmiers, twists, etc.)
16 miniature vanilla-flavored meringues

The Little Bowls

1 bowl dried grated coconut
1 bowl unsweetened cocoa powder
1 bowl granulated sugar

1 bowl grilled slivered almonds (see p. 118)
1 bowl ground cinnamon

The Sauce

14 ounces (400 g) semisweet chocolate
2 cups (½ l) warm water
1 pinch salt
1 stick plus 1 tablespoon (125 g) butter, cut into 8 pieces

PREPARATION TIME

The fruit—20 to 25 minutes; the sauce—10 to 12 minutes

Procedure

Prepare all of the fruits and reserve, each one in a separate bowl, in the refrigerator.

Cut each slice of buttered toast into 4 equal squares. Pile on a plate and place on the table.

Cut or break the lady fingers, vanilla wafers, and puff pastry cookies in half, place each one, as well as the meringues, on a separate plate and arrange on the table.

Arrange the little bowls of coconut, cocoa, sugar, almonds, and cinnamon on the table.

To make the sauce: Place the chocolate, ½ cup (120 ml) of the water, and the salt in a saucepan and melt as described on page 29. Stir until smooth and creamy, then stir in the butter, a piece at a time. Continue stirring until thick and smooth, then, little by little, stir in the rest of the water and bring to a boil; as soon as the sauce thickens, remove from the heat and place in a chafing dish in the middle of the table.

Remove the fruits from the refrigerator and arrange them on the table. Now the fondue is ready to eat as described on page 86.

Winter Fondue

FONDUE D'HIVER

INGREDIENTS FOR 8 SERVINGS

The Dry Elements

4 to 5 slices toast, buttered
3 thick slices fruit cake
3 thick slices brioche or egg
 bread
16 tiny butter cookies or 8
 medium ones, broken in half

The Crêpe Batter

½ cup (70 g) flour
1 pinch salt
1 whole egg
½ cup (120 ml) milk
1½ teaspoons cooking oil
1½ teaspoons dark rum
 (optional)
Butter (to grease pan)

The Fruits

24 tangerine sections, white
 strings removed
2 to 3 slices canned pineapple,
 cut into 8 wedges each
2 large bananas, cut into slices
 a good ½ inch (1.5 cm) thick,
 mixed with the juice of 1
 lemon (to prevent
 discoloration)
⅔ cup (125 g) raisins, soaked 30
 minutes in a mixture of 2
 tablespoons hot water and 2
 tablespoons dark rum, then
 drained
8 strips candied orange peel

The Little Bowls

1 bowl dried grated coconut
1 bowl unsweetened cocoa
 powder

1 bowl grated chocolate
1 bowl ground cinnamon

The Sauce

14 ounces (400 g) semisweet
 chocolate
1 pinch salt
1⅔ cups (400 ml) heavy cream
5 tablespoons (75 g) butter, cut
 into 5 pieces and allowed to
 soften
6 tablespoons (75 g) granulated
 sugar
2 tablespoons whiskey

PREPARATION TIME

*The fruits—25 to 30 minutes;
the crêpes—15 to 20 minutes;
the sauce—10 to 12 minutes*

Procedure

Prepare the tangerine sections, pineapple, and bananas, and place in separate bowls in the refrigerator.

Soak and drain the raisins, cut the candied peel in half, and place in separate bowls on the table.

Cut each slice of buttered toast into 4 equal squares. Pile onto a small plate and place on the table.

Cut the fruit cake and brioche or egg bread into bite-sized pieces. Place on separate plates on the table; put the cookies on a plate as well.

To make the crêpes: In a large frying pan, make tiny crêpes, 4 to 6 at a time, as described on page 83. Use only 1 teaspoon of batter for each one, and spread it out with the back of the spoon, leaving plenty of space between them; make about 24 of them in all, keeping each batch warm in the oven while making the next one.

Place the little bowls of coconut, cocoa, grated chocolate, and cinnamon on the table.

To make the sauce: Place the chocolate, salt, and cream in a saucepan and melt over very low heat as described on page 29. When melted, stir in the butter, piece by piece, then stir in the sugar and whiskey. Continue stirring for 2 to 3 minutes to melt the sugar and make a perfectly smooth sauce.

Place the fruits and crêpes on the table and pour the sauce in a chafing dish; the fondue is ready to eat as described on page 86.

Chocolate Omelet with Vanilla Ice Cream

OMELETTE AU CHOCOLAT, GLACE À LA VANILLE

INGREDIENTS FOR 4 SERVINGS

½ *pint (¼ l) vanilla ice cream*
4 egg yolks
¼ *cup (50 g) granulated sugar*
2 tablespoons (20 g)
  unsweetened cocoa powder
1 pinch ground cinnamon
4 egg whites
2 tablespoons (30 g) butter
Confectioners' sugar

 his dessert is made just before serving.

Procedure

About 20 minutes before making the omelet, transfer the ice cream from the freezer to the refrigerator so that it won't be too hard.

Place the egg yolks in a mixing bowl with half of the sugar. Beat until pale in color, thick, and creamy. Stir in the cocoa and cinnamon.

In a separate mixing bowl, beat the egg whites until thick and beginning to increase in volume, then sprinkle the rest of the sugar over them and beat until firm and shiny. Fold this into the egg yolk–cocoa mixture.

Melt the butter in a large frying pan over moderately low heat; when it no longer sizzles, pour in the omelet mixture all at once and cook, shaking the pan constantly back and forth over the heat to allow the eggs to set without sticking. The outside (bottom) should be firm and lightly crisp, but the inside should be creamy.

Remove the pan from the heat and rapidly spoon the ice cream over half of it. With a flexible-blade metal spatula, fold the other half over it. Slide the omelet onto a serving platter, sprinkle lightly with confectioners' sugar, and serve immediately.

Comments: The omelet must be garnished and served very quickly, because, although the ice cream should melt a little bit from the heat of the omelet, it should not melt completely.

If you prefer, a nut brittle ice cream or caramel ice cream may be used instead of the vanilla.

Rum Omelet with Rum-Coffee Fudge Sauce

OMELETTE AU RHUM, FUDGE DE CHOCOLAT, RHUM ET CAFÉ

The sauce may be made in advance and reheated in a double boiler. The omelet must be made just before serving.

Procedure

Make the Rum-Coffee Fudge Sauce and allow to cook while making the omelet (or make in advance and reheat).

In a mixing bowl, beat the egg yolks and sugar until very pale in color, creamy, and smooth. Stir in the rum.

In a separate mixing bowl, beat the egg whites and salt until very stiff, then fold into the egg yolks.

Melt the butter over moderate heat; when it no longer sizzles, pour the omelet mixture into the pan all at once. As the edges cook, pull them into the center of the pan with a flexible-blade metal spatula, going round and round the pan, and tipping the pan toward the uncovered edge to cover it with uncooked batter. When all of the batter has begun to set, leave the omelet alone, but shake the pan gently back and forth to keep it from sticking. When done, the bottom should be golden brown and slightly crisp, the top still creamy.

INGREDIENTS FOR 4 SERVINGS

Rum-Coffee Fudge Sauce
  (p. 122)
5 egg yolks
¼ cup (50 g) granulated sugar
1 tablespoon dark rum
6 egg whites
1 pinch salt
2 tablespoons (30 g) butter

PREPARATION TIME

The sauce—20 minutes; the omelet—12 to 15 minutes

Turn the omelet out onto a serving platter by sliding it halfway out of the pan, then flipping the second half over it with a quick lifting and pushing motion of the edge of the pan. Surround the folded omelet with the sauce and serve immediately.

Snow Eggs with Chocolate-Caramel Custard Sauce

OEUFS À LA NEIGE, CRÈME AU CHOCOLAT CARAMÉLISÉ

INGREDIENTS FOR 6 SERVINGS

Chocolate-Caramel Custard Sauce (p. 124)
6 egg whites
⅞ cup (175 g) granulated sugar
Unsweetened cocoa powder

PREPARATION TIME

The sauce—30 to 35 minutes; the snow eggs—5 to 10 minutes, plus 7 minutes' cooking per batch

The custard sauce should be made well in advance in order to have time to chill (it should be served very cold). The snow eggs may be made 2 to 3 hours before serving.

Procedure

Make the Chocolate-Caramel Custard Sauce and reserve it in the refrigerator. Since the sauce uses only the egg yolks, reserve the whites in a closed container until ready to make the snow eggs.

To make the snow eggs: Fill a large *sauteuse* or high-sided frying pan with water. Heat until simmering.

In a mixing bowl, beat the egg whites until very stiff, then fold in the sugar.

Spread a large sheet of waxed paper on the table and sprinkle with a little water. With a serving spoon, make 12 large egg-shaped mounds of egg white; set them down on the waxed paper. When all the "eggs" are made, lift them off the paper, one by one, with a flexible-blade metal spatula and place them upside down in the simmering water. They should not touch, so you will probably have to cook them in 3 to 4 batches. Poach for 5 minutes on the first side, then turn the "eggs" over and poach 2 minutes on the second side.

Spread a large dish towel out on the table. When the "eggs" have finished poaching, lift them out of the water with a skimmer or slotted spoon and set them down to drain.

Pour the custard sauce into a large serving dish and carefully set the snow eggs on top. Just before serving, sprinkle with cocoa as described on page 117 and serve.

Note: If preferred, the snow eggs may be served on individual dessert plates. In this case, after draining, place them on a large plate until ready to serve. To serve, spoon the sauce onto the plates, set 2 snow eggs in the center of each, sprinkle with cocoa, and serve. Ed.

Chocolate Pudding

PETITS POTS DE CRÈME

This is a wonderful old-fashioned dessert, easy to make. It can be eaten either warm or cold.

Procedure

Preheat the oven to 350°F (175°C).

Place the milk and sugar in a saucepan and bring almost to a boil. Place the cocoa in a mixing bowl, and, little by little, whisk the hot milk into it.

In another mixing bowl, beat the eggs as if for scrambled eggs. Slowly whisk the chocolate milk into them. Rinse out the bowl the chocolate milk was in and strain the mixture back into it (this is to eliminate any lumps of egg white).

Fill 6 individual custard dishes with the chocolate mixture and set them in a large casserole or stew pot. Pour enough boiling water into the casserole to come ⅔ of the way up the sides of the custard dishes. Cover the casserole and place in the oven to bake for 1 hour, or until a trussing needle inserted in the center of a pudding comes out clean.

Remove the casserole from the oven, uncover it, and allow the puddings to cool to warm in the water, then remove them from the casserole and allow to cool to room temperature. Serve at room temperature, or, if you prefer, slightly warm.

INGREDIENTS FOR 6
SERVINGS

1 quart (1 l) milk
¼ cup (50 g) granulated sugar
¼ cup (40 g) unsweetened cocoa
  powder
6 whole eggs

PREPARATION TIME

1 hour 15 minutes

Spice Pudding

PUDDING AUX ÉPICES

Be sure to make the custard sauce well in advance so that it will have time to cool and chill. The pudding can be eaten either warm or cold.

Procedure

Make the Vanilla Custard Sauce well in advance and reserve in the refrigerator.

Preheat the oven to 350°F (175°C).

Take a baking dish or roasting pan large enough to hold an 8½-inch-wide (22 cm) soufflé mold and pour in water to a depth of about ½ inch (1 cm). Place in the oven.

Vanilla Custard Sauce (p. 124)
¾ *cup (150 g) granulated sugar*
¼ *pound (110 g) butter,*
  softened
½ *cup (80 g) flour*
½ *teaspoon instant coffee*
¼ *teaspoon ground cinnamon*
¼ *teaspoon ground allspice*
1 pinch nutmeg
5¼ *ounces (150 g) semisweet*
  chocolate
½ *cup (120 ml) milk*
5 eggs, separated
1 pinch salt

PREPARATION TIME

The pudding—1 to 1½ hours;
the sauce—15 to 20 minutes

Butter the soufflé mold generously, then pour in about ¼ cup of the sugar. Tip and turn the mold in all directions to coat the bottom and sides with the sugar (add more sugar if necessary), then pour out any excess and place the mold in the refrigerator.

In a mixing bowl, beat the butter and the remaining ½ cup (100 g) sugar together until smooth and creamy.

In another bowl, mix the flour, coffee, and spices, then stir this mixture into the butter. When the mixture is perfectly smooth and of a uniform color, reserve.

In a saucepan, melt the chocolate as described on page 29 in 3 tablespoons of the milk. Stir until perfectly smooth, slowly stir in the rest of the milk, then raise the heat and heat just until the chocolate milk begins to bubble around the edges. Remove from the heat and stir slowly into the spice-butter mixture.

When well mixed, pour back into the saucepan and place over moderate heat. Bring to a boil, stirring constantly, then cook, stirring energetically, for 1 to 2 minutes, or until the dough detaches itself from the sides of the saucepan.

Remove from the heat and stir in the egg yolks one at a time, making sure that each one is completely mixed in before adding the next one.

Beat the egg whites and salt until very stiff, then fold ⅓ of them into the chocolate dough. When completely mixed in, fold in the remaining egg whites without working the mixture too much—it's perfectly all right, even preferable, if there are unmixed traces of egg white or dough in the finished batter.

Pour the batter into the soufflé mold and smooth the surface with a spoon or spatula. Place the mold in the baking dish with the water and bake for 35 to 40 minutes, or until a knife blade inserted in the center comes out clean.

Remove from the oven and allow to cool for 5 minutes. Then run the blade of a knife all around the edge of the pudding, place a serving platter upside down on top of the mold, and turn everything over. Shake firmly and set on the table with a firm tap, then lift off the mold.

Allow to cool, either to warm or to room temperature, and serve with a sauceboat of Vanilla Custard Sauce.

Comment: If you prefer, you may serve this pudding with Whipped Cream with Grated Chocolate (p. 126) instead of the Vanilla Custard Sauce.

Date-Nut Pudding

PUDDING AUX DATTES ET AUX AMANDES

Both the pudding and sauce are made in advance; the sauce is reheated just before serving.

Procedure

Preheat the oven to 350°F (175°C).

Coarsely chop the slivered almonds and place them in a bowl with the grated chocolate.

Place the chopped dates in a sieve and sprinkle with the flour. With your fingers, mix the flour and dates together in order to separate the pieces of date from each other and make them less sticky. When done, shake the sieve to eliminate any excess flour.

Add the dates to the almonds and chocolate; stir to mix, and reserve.

In a mixing bowl, place the egg yolks, vanilla extract, and sugar. Beat until pale in color and very thick and creamy.

Mix the remaining flour and the baking powder together and stir into the egg yolk mixture, then stir in the cream. Pour into the bowl with the dates, almonds, and chocolate, and mix together well to distribute them evenly throughout the batter.

In a separate mixing bowl, beat the egg whites and salt together until very stiff, then fold ⅓ into the batter. When well mixed, fold in the remaining egg whites.

Butter a 7-inch (18 cm) soufflé mold, pour in the batter, and bake for 35 to 40 minutes, or until a knife blade inserted in the center comes out clean.

While the pudding is baking, make the Hot Chocolate Sauce.

When done, remove the pudding from the oven and allow to cool completely. Just before serving, sprinkle with cocoa as described on page 117 and reheat the chocolate sauce. Serve the pudding in the soufflé mold with the sauce in a sauceboat on the side.

INGREDIENTS FOR 6 To 8 SERVINGS

½ cup (40 g) slivered almonds
4¼ ounces (125 g) semisweet chocolate, grated
½ cup (100 g) chopped dates
2 tablespoons (20 g) flour (for the dates)
3 egg yolks
½ teaspoon vanilla extract
½ cup (100 g) granulated sugar
2 tablespoons (20 g) flour (for the pudding)
1 teaspoon baking powder
6 ½ tablespoons (100 ml) heavy cream
3 egg whites
1 pinch salt
Hot Chocolate Sauce (p. 120)
Unsweetened cocoa powder

PREPARATION TIME

The pudding—1 hour 40 minutes; the sauce—10 to 15 minutes

Steamed Chocolate-Nut Pudding

PUDDING À L'ÉTOUFFÉ DE NOIX ET DE CAFÉ

The sauce should be made well in advance because it is served cold. Begin cooking the pudding about 2 hours ahead of time, so that it can be served hot.

Coffee Custard Sauce (p. 124)
1 teaspoon instant coffee
2 tablespoons hot water
5¼ ounces (150 g) semisweet chocolate
4 tablespoons (60 g) butter, softened
½ cup (100 g) granulated sugar
2 whole eggs, lightly beaten
1⅔ cups (225 g) flour
2 teaspoons baking powder
1 pinch salt
¾ cup (175 ml) milk
⅔ cup (60 g) chopped walnuts

PREPARATION TIME

The sauce—15 to 20 minutes; the pudding—40 to 45 minutes for the batter, 1 ½ hours to cook

Procedure

Make the Coffee Custard Sauce well in advance and reserve in the refrigerator.

Dissolve the instant coffee in the hot water, then add the chocolate and melt over very low heat as described on page 29. Stir until perfectly smooth, then remove from the heat.

In a mixing bowl, beat the butter and sugar together until smooth and creamy, using a wooden spoon. Stir in the beaten eggs, ⅓ at a time to make a smooth, creamy mixture.

Mix the flour, baking powder, and salt together in a bowl. Stir ⅓ of it into the egg-butter mixture, then ⅓ of the milk, and continue in this way alternating the flour and milk, ⅓ at a time. When the batter is perfectly smooth, stir in the melted chocolate and the walnuts.

Butter a soufflé mold 7 inches (18 cm) in diameter. Pour in the batter, smooth the surface with a spoon or spatula, then cover the mold with a sheet of aluminum foil. Press the foil tightly against the sides of the mold. Run 2 pieces of strong adhesive tape across the top of the foil and down onto the sides of the mold, perpendicular to each other, then run tape all around the mold to stick the foil tightly in place and seal the mold completely closed.

Place the soufflé mold in a large pot and pour in enough hot water to come halfway up the sides of the mold. Cover the pot, place over moderate heat, and bring the water to a boil. Lower the heat and allow the pudding to simmer for 1½ hours.

Remove the pudding from the pot and set it on a cake rack to cool for 10 minutes before opening it. To serve, remove the tape and foil, then serve hot in the soufflé mold, with a sauceboat of Coffee Custard Sauce on the side.

Puff Pastry Orange Fritters with Orange-Flavored Chocolate Sauce

RISSOLES D'ORANGES À LA SAUCE CHOCOLAT À L'ORANGE

The oranges must steep in syrup for 1 to 2 hours, so take this into account when making this dessert.

Procedure

Make the Puff Pastry dough, or, if made in advance and frozen, remove from the freezer and place in the refrigerator to thaw, several hours in advance.

Place the sugar, water, and wine in a saucepan, bring to a boil, and allow to simmer for 3 to 4 minutes to make a syrup. Drop the orange sections into the boiling syrup, remove immediately from the heat, and allow to sit for 1 to 2 hours before using. At the end of this time, lift out the orange sections using a skimmer or slotted spoon and drain them on a clean dish towel.

Roll out the puff pastry very thin and, using a 3½-inch (9 cm) round cookie cutter (a large glass or cup may be used if you don't have a cookie cutter), cut out 24 circles. Place an orange section on ½ of each circle, then fold the other half of the dough over it and crimp the edges to enclose the oranges completely and make miniature turnovers. Set aside.

Make the Orange-Flavored Chocolate Sauce and keep warm over low heat.

Heat the oil in a deep fryer to 350°F (175°C). While it is heating, spread out paper towels to drain the fritters on. Drop the fritters into the hot oil and fry until golden brown—this should take only 2 to 3 minutes each. To avoid crowding, you will have to fry in 2 to 3 batches, depending on the size of your deep fryer. Drain the fritters on the paper towels, then place on a serving platter (keep warm in a very low oven, if necessary). When all of the fritters are done, serve, with a sauceboat of the chocolate-orange sauce on the side.

INGREDIENTS FOR 6 SERVINGS

10½ ounces (300 g) Puff Pastry dough (p. 66)
2 cups (400 g) granulated sugar
2 cups (½ l) water
1 cup (¼ l) dry white wine
24 orange sections, membranes removed (see p. 71)
Orange-Flavored Chocolate Sauce (p. 121)
Deep-frying oil

PREPARATION TIME

The fritters—40 to 50 minutes; the sauce—20 minutes

Chocolate "Soup" with French-Toast "Croutons"

SOUPE DE CHOCOLAT AU PAIN PERDU

The sauce may be made in advance and reheated in a double boiler, but the French toast must be made at the last minute.

Procedure

Make the Hot Chocolate Sauce and keep warm, or make in advance and reheat.

In a bowl, mix the sugar and cinnamon together.

Place the pieces of bread in a large shallow dish and pour the warm milk over them. After 1 to 2 minutes, turn them over to soak the other side. Although the bread should be moist, it should not be soggy. Place on a cake rack to drain.

INGREDIENTS FOR 6 SERVINGS

Hot Chocolate Sauce (p. 120)
¼ cup (50 g) granulated sugar
1 teaspoon ground cinnamon
5 slices country-style bread, crusts removed
¾ cup (200 ml) milk, warmed
3 whole eggs
4 tablespoons (60 g) butter

*The sauce—10 to 15 minutes;
the French toast—10 to 15
minutes*

Preheat the oven to warm, and place 6 soup plates inside.

In another soup plate or shallow dish, lightly beat the eggs.

Place 2 frying pans (to make things go faster) over moderate heat and melt the butter in them. Quickly dip the bread in the eggs, first one side then the other, and put them in the sizzling butter. Brown on one side, then turn over to brown the other (don't cook too fast, or the butter will burn). Remove from the butter, place on a cutting board, and sprinkle with the cinnamon-sugar.

With a serrated knife, cut each slice of French toast into 6 pieces. Remove the soup plates from the oven and place 5 pieces of toast in each one, with the cinnamon-sugar facing up. Pour the chocolate sauce in between the pieces of French toast to completely cover the bottom of the soup plates (the "croutons" should look as if they are floating), and serve immediately.

Chocolate Soufflé

SOUFFLÉ AU CHOCOLAT

INGREDIENTS FOR 6 SERVINGS

*5¼ ounces (150 g) semisweet
    chocolate
3 tablespoons (50 ml) water
4 egg yolks
6 tablespoons (75 g) granulated
    sugar
½ teaspoon ground cinnamon
6 egg whites
1 pinch salt*

PREPARATION TIME

20 to 30 minutes

U nlike a traditional soufflé, this one contains no flour. It is made at the last minute and served hot from the oven.

Procedure

Preheat the oven to 425°F (220°C).

Place the chocolate and water in a saucepan and melt over very low heat as described on page 29. Remove from the heat.

In a mixing bowl, beat the egg yolks and sugar together until very pale in color and creamy. Stir in the chocolate and cinnamon.

In a separate mixing bowl, beat the egg whites and salt until very stiff. Fold ½ the whites into the chocolate mixture until a uniform color and texture is obtained, then fold in the rest. It is perfectly all right, even preferable, if the final mixture is slightly uneven in color.

Butter a 2- to 2½-quart (2 to 2½ l) oval baking dish. (Do *not* use a soufflé mold.) Pour in the batter and spread it out smooth (it will only be about 1 inch [2.5 cm] thick). Bake in the middle of the oven for 10 to 12 minutes, or just long enough for the soufflé to have risen to about twice its original height. As soon as it has stopped rising, remove from the oven and serve immediately.

Baked in this way, the soufflé is hot, but not really cooked—that's the way I like it. If you prefer your soufflé "done," simply prolong the cooking time until the blade of a knife inserted in the center comes out clean. It's all a question of taste.

4

Mini-Desserts and Candies

MINI-DESSERTS

T hese mini-pastries and candies are for nibblers. You can nibble on them in the afternoon, or with coffee after dinner, or anytime you like.

It's a little hard to classify them, because some of them fall somewhere between pastries and candies. But they are all easy to make if you take the pains to measure out all the ingredients and have all the utensils ready to use and at hand before starting.

Pineapple Tidbits

BOUCHÉES À L'ANANAS

INGREDIENTS FOR 16 TIDBITS

1½ cups (125 g) slivered
   almonds
¾ cup (125 g) confectioners'
   sugar
5 tablespoons (75 g) butter,
   softened (for the tidbits)
1 tablespoon pineapple juice
   (from the canned pineapple)
1 teaspoon dark rum
2 slices canned pineapple
3½ ounces (100 g) semisweet
   chocolate
2½ tablespoons (40 g) butter
   (for the chocolate)

T hese should be made a day in advance and kept in a cool place (but not in the refrigerator).

Procedure

Brown the slivered almonds as described on page 118. Chop them coarsely, then sift the confectioners' sugar over them and stir together.

In a mixing bowl, beat the butter until very soft and creamy. Stir in the almond-sugar mixture, the pineapple juice, and the rum. When mixed together, beat with a wooden spoon to make the mixture thick and smooth. With your fingers, form the mixture into 16 little balls; spread them out on a platter and place in the refrigerator to set.

Drain the pineapple slices and pat dry in a clean dish towel or cloth. Cut into 16 wedges and reserve.

In a double boiler, melt the chocolate and butter together. When melted, stir until smooth, then remove from the heat and allow to cool almost completely.

Remove the little balls from the refrigerator, and, holding each one carefully between your thumb and index finger, dip them one by one into the chocolate to coat them halfway. Set them on a baking sheet, chocolate side down, and leave until the chocolate has hardened.

Set 16 little paper cases (optional) on a serving platter and put a tidbit in each one, chocolate side up. Lightly press a pineapple wedge onto each one, then put in a cool place (out of the refrigerator) until you serve them the next day.

PREPARATION TIME

50 minutes

Cocoa Balls

CACAO-BOULES

These little round cookies are crunchy on the outside, soft and creamy on the inside. They keep well in a tightly closed cookie box, and are delicious with coffee.

Procedure

Preheat the oven to 325°F (160°C).

Sift the flour, cocoa, salt, and cinnamon into a bowl.

Place the butter in a mixing bowl and beat in the confectioners' sugar and vanilla extract little by little. When the mixture is creamy and pale in color, stir in the sifted flour-cocoa mixture little by little to form a stiff dough. Form the dough into a ball, then flatten it slightly on the table and cut it into 4 pieces. Form each one of these pieces into a ball, flatten it, and cut it into 12 pieces, making a total of 48.

Line a baking sheet with waxed paper. Roll each little piece of dough into a ball and place them on the baking sheet, leaving space between them because they will spread a little. Bake for 12 to 14 minutes, or until the tops have browned, turning the baking sheet around halfway through the cooking time if the cookies seem to be browning unevenly.

Remove from the oven and allow to cool completely on the baking sheet (they are too soft to handle when hot). When perfectly cold, detach them from the waxed paper and serve, or put into a tightly closed cookie box for later use.

INGREDIENTS FOR 48 COOKIES

Generous 1 1/2 cups (220 g) flour
6 tablespoons (60 g)
*   unsweetened cocoa powder*
1 pinch salt
1/2 teaspoon ground cinnamon
1/2 pound (225 g) butter,
*   softened*
6 tablespoons (60 g)
*   confectioners' sugar, sifted*
*   after measuring*
1 teaspoon vanilla extract

PREPARATION TIME

50 to 60 minutes

Hazelnut Tidbits

BOUCHÉES AUX NOISETTES

INGREDIENTS FOR
ABOUT 16 TO 20
TIDBITS

4¼ ounces (125 g) semisweet
  chocolate
2 tablespoons water
2 tablespoons crème fraîche
  (p. 30) or heavy cream
1 cup (125 g) ground hazelnuts
⅞ cup (130 g) confectioners'
  sugar
1 tablespoon whiskey
Unsweetened cocoa powder
16 to 20 golden raisins

PREPARATION TIME

30 minutes, plus 3 hours resting
time

Although these are easy to make, the mixture must chill for 3 hours before being formed into balls, so be sure to take this into account.

Procedure

Place the chocolate and water in a saucepan and melt as described on page 29. Stir until smooth and creamy, then add the cream, ground hazelnuts, confectioners' sugar, and whiskey. Stir vigorously to make a thick, uniform mixture. Place in the refrigerator for 3 hours to chill and stiffen.

With your fingers, form little balls. Roll them in the cocoa powder, place in little paper cases on a serving platter, press a raisin into the top of each one, and serve.

Chocolate Cups Filled with Tangerine Jelly

COUPELLES DE CHOCOLAT À LA GELÉE DE CLÉMENTINE

INGREDIENTS FOR 12
to 16 CUPS

9 ounces (250 g) semisweet
  chocolate
6 tablespoons (100 ml) freshly
  squeezed tangerine juice
12 to 16 fresh tangerine sections
⅔ cup (125 g) granulated sugar
¾ cup (175 ml) water
2¼ teaspoons granulated
  unflavored gelatin softened
  in 7 teaspoons cold water, or 3
  sheets softened in a bowl of
  cold water
2 egg whites, very lightly beaten

These are a little complicated to make, but wonderfully fresh to eat.

Procedure

To make the chocolate cups: You will need smooth-sided, round petit-four molds, 1¼ to 1½ inches (3 to 4 cm) wide. Line each one with a piece of aluminum foil that sticks out over the edge of the mold.

Melt the chocolate in a double boiler as described on page 29. When completely soft, stir until smooth. Remove from the heat and allow to cool to lukewarm.

Place 1 teaspoon of chocolate in each mold, tipping and turning to make it coat the sides; use your finger, if necessary, to spread it around and smooth out the layer of chocolate. Coat the molds one at a time and place in the refrigerator to harden as soon as each one is done.

To make the jelly: While the chocolate is hardening, strain the tangerine juice through several layers of cheesecloth or other clean cloth; reserve.

Remove any white strings from the tangerine sections.

Place the sugar, water, gelatin (if using sheets, drain before adding), tangerine juice, and egg whites in a saucepan over moderately low heat and bring slowly to a boil. Whisk constantly, making sure that the sugar and gelatin melt completely. As soon as the mixture begins to boil, remove from the heat.

Strain the liquid through a clean cloth or several layers of cheesecloth into a bowl. The strained liquid should be very clear. Allow to cool to room temperature.

When the liquid has cooled completely, but not yet begun to set, remove the molds from the refrigerator and place a tangerine section in each one. Pour in enough liquid to cover the tangerine, and place back into the refrigerator to set the jelly.

To serve: lift the little cups out of the molds by holding on to the aluminum foil. Carefully peel off the foil and set the cups down on a serving platter. If not serving immediately, put back into the refrigerator until ready to serve.

PREPARATION TIME

The chocolate cups—30 to 35 minutes; the jelly—10 to 15 minutes

Toll House Cookies

GALETTES D'OCTROI (RECETTE AMÉRICAINE)

This is *the* American cookie, and I find them absolutely delicious. What amazes me is that the bits of chocolate, strangely, don't melt while baking but remain crunchy.

Procedure

Preheat the oven to 475°F (250°C).

Place the chocolate bar on a cutting board and chop it coarsely, using a large, sharp knife and rocking the blade back and forth by pressing down on the handle with one hand, on the end of the blade with the other. Reserve on a plate.

Place the butter, white sugar, and light brown sugar in a mixing bowl. Beat until creamy and light in color.

In a smaller bowl, lightly beat the egg with the water, then stir this into the butter mixture.

Sift the flour, salt, and baking soda together and stir, little by little, into the butter-egg mixture. Beat with the spoon to form a

INGREDIENTS FOR 40 TO 45 COOKIES

One 7-ounce (200 g) semisweet chocolate bar (or two 3½-ounce [100 g] bars)
1 stick plus 1 tablespoon (125 g) butter, softened
6 tablespoons (75 g) granulated sugar
6 tablespoons (60 g) light brown sugar
1 whole egg
¼ teaspoon water
1 ¾ cups (250 g) flour
½ teaspoon salt
½ teaspoon baking soda

smooth mixture, then stir in the chopped chocolate. Make sure the chocolate chips are evenly distributed in the dough.

Butter a baking sheet and, using an ordinary teaspoon, drop little mounds of the dough onto it, leaving at least an inch (2.5 cm) between the mounds, because they will spread while baking. Bake for 10 minutes, or until just golden brown. Remove from the oven, allow to cool, then remove from the baking sheet.

Shiny Chocolate Madeleines

MADELEINES VERNIES AU CHOCOLAT

INGREDIENTS FOR ABOUT 24 LARGE MADELEINES (12 SERVINGS)

The Chocolate Mousse

3½ ounces (100 g) semisweet chocolate
2 tablespoons water
2 tablespoons (30 g) butter, cut into 2 pieces and allowed to soften
1 large egg yolk
1½ egg whites (to equal ¼ cup)
1 pinch salt

The Madeleines

2¾ ounces (75 g) semisweet chocolate
10 tablespoons (140 g) butter, cut into 8 pieces and allowed to soften
2 tablespoons (20 g) unsweetened cocoa powder
⅞ cup (175 g) granulated sugar
1⅛ cups (150 g) flour
1 pinch salt
3 whole eggs
2 egg yolks
½ teaspoon vanilla extract

T his dessert can be made 2 to 3 hours in advance, the madeleines and mousse several hours ahead of time.

Procedure

To make the chocolate mousse: Follow the instructions given on page 32 and place in the refrigerator.

Preheat the oven to 350°F (175°C).

Lightly butter the madeleine molds.

To make the madeleines: Place the chocolate and butter in a saucepan and melt over low heat, stirring until smooth and shiny.

Sift the cocoa, sugar, flour, and salt together into a saucepan. In a mixing bowl, beat the eggs and extra egg yolks together as for scrambled eggs, then whisk in the vanilla extract.

Little by little, stir the chocolate-butter mixture into the flour-cocoa mixture. When well mixed together, stir in the eggs, ⅓ at a time. Place the saucepan over very low heat and cook, stirring constantly, until just warm to the touch. The mixture will become smoother and slightly easier to stir.

Take the madeleine molds and fill each one halfway—if using large molds, this means using about a tablespoonful of batter for each one. Shake very gently to level out the batter, then place in the oven and bake for 12 minutes, or until a knife inserted in the center of one comes out clean (the madeleines should have doubled in size).

Remove from the oven and turn out onto a sheet of parchment paper or a cake rack. Allow to cool.

To assemble the dessert: Make the chocolate icing according to the instructions given on page 115 and allow to cool to warm (it should be relatively thick).

Take a madeleine and spread about 1 tablespoonful of mousse on the smooth side; it should be somewhat thicker at the wide end than at the narrow one. Take a second madeleine and stick it to the first one, smooth side down, pressing the narrow ends together. The shell design will be on the outside. With a pastry brush, ice the top madeleine, spreading the icing in the direction of the grooves (see photo following p. 104). Set the finished madeleine dessert (the bottom madeleine remains uniced) on a serving platter, and continue making the desserts, one at a time, in the same way.

If you are making the desserts in advance, they may be placed in the refrigerator, but be sure to remove them and leave them at room temperature for at least 30 minutes before serving so that the icing, which dulls in the refrigerator, can become shiny again.

Note: Madeleine molds typically come in sheets of 12; if you have 2 sheets, you can bake all of the madeleines at once. If not, bake in 2 batches, stirring the batter to make it smooth before filling the molds for the second time.

Semisweet chocolate may be substituted for coating chocolate, but the madeleines will not be as glossy. Ed.

The Chocolate Icing

1¾ ounces (50 g) coating chocolate (p. 21; see note)
1 tablespoon water
1 pinch salt
1½ tablespoons (20 g) butter, broken into 2 pieces and allowed to soften

PREPARATION TIME

The mousse—30 to 35 minutes; the madeleines—45 to 50 minutes; the icing—10 minutes

Chocolate Meringue Fingers

DOIGTS DE MERINGUE AU CHOCOLAT

Meringues keep a long time if placed in a tightly covered cookie box, so you can make these whenever you have time.

Procedure

Preheat the oven to 250°F (120°C).

Place the sugar and egg whites in a mixing bowl. Set the bowl in a larger bowl of very hot, but not boiling water and beat until thick and foamy and almost doubled in volume. Remove from the heat and continue beating until very stiff.

Sprinkle the cocoa over the beaten egg whites and fold it in; the finished mixture should be of a uniform color.

Butter a baking sheet. Using a pastry bag equipped with a ⅜-inch (1 cm) nozzle, squeeze out little fingers of the meringue (if you don't have a pastry bag, you can use a teaspoon). Bake for 45 minutes, keeping the oven door slightly ajar by inserting the handle of a wooden spoon. When the meringues are done, they should be dry on the outside, but still slightly moist on the inside. Remove from

INGREDIENTS FOR ABOUT 30 MERINGUES

¾ cup (150 g) granulated sugar
3 egg whites
2 tablespoons (20 g) unsweetened cocoa powder

PREPARATION TIME

About 1 hour to 1 hour 15 minutes

the oven, allow to cool completely, then remove from the baking sheet.

Variation

You can make double meringues by sticking them together with butter cream. Make a Chocolate Butter Cream (p. 125) and spread a layer of it on the flat side of a meringue. Stick the flat side of another meringue to the butter cream, pressing lightly. Place the double meringues in little paper cases and serve on a serving platter.

Although the meringues can be made well in advance and stored in a cookie box, the butter cream should be made and spread on them just before serving.

Mini–Chocolate Éclairs

MINI-ÉCLAIRS AU CHOCOLAT

INGREDIENTS FOR
ABOUT 20 MINI-
ÉCLAIRS

½ recipe Cream Puff Pastry
   dough (p. 72)
1⅔ cups (400 g) Chocolate
   Pastry Cream (p. 36)
½ recipe Simple Chocolate
   Icing (p. 115)

PREPARATION TIME

*The pastries—30 to 40 minutes;
the pastry cream—20 to 30
minutes; the icing—10 minutes*

The pastries and pastry cream may be made a day in advance, but éclairs should be filled the day they are to be eaten because they quickly become soggy.

Procedure

Preheat the oven to 400°F (200°C).

Make the Cream Puff Pastry dough. Line a baking sheet with waxed paper and, using a pastry bag fitted with a ⅜-inch (1 cm) nozzle, squeeze out little finger-sized pastries. Bake for 15 to 20 minutes, or until golden brown. Remove from the oven and allow to cool.

While the pastries are baking, make the Chocolate Pastry Cream.

To fill the éclairs, slit them open along one side and, using a pastry bag or a spoon, fill them with the pastry cream.

Make the Simple Chocolate Icing. When it has cooled to warm and thickened slightly, ice the éclairs using a butter knife. Keep in a cool place until ready to serve.

Chocolate Meringue Fingers and Florentines (pages 103, 105)

Shiny Chocolate Madeleines and Chocolate Tile Cookies
(pages 102, 107)

Icing a Cake (page 114)

Chocolate Shavings (page 117)

Florentines

FLORENTINS

Florentines fall somewhere between cookies and candies. They can be made several days in advance if kept in a tightly closed metal or plastic box in a cool, dry place (not in the refrigerator).

Procedure

Preheat the oven to 400°F (200°C).

Place the sugar and honey in a saucepan. Stir in 4 tablespoons of the water and bring to a boil. Cook to the "soft-ball stage" (240° to 244°F [115° to 118°C] on a candy thermometer), when a little of the boiling syrup dropped from a teaspoon into a glass of ice water can be formed into a soft ball between your fingers. Stir in the cream, the candied fruits, and the almonds. Mix well together with a wooden spoon to form a thick, sticky mixture.

Take some nonstick tartlet molds 2¾ to 3½ inches (7 to 9 cm) in diameter. Using 2 ordinary tablespoons, place about a tablespoonful of the mixture in each mold, scraping it from one of the spoons with the other. Moisten a spoon to flatten the mound and help cover the bottom of the mold. Bake for about 10 minutes, or until the edges of the mixture have caramelized.

Remove from the oven and allow to cool almost completely but not enough to harden. Remove the almond-caramel disks from the molds with a small spatula and place on a cake rack to harden competely.

Melt the chocolate with the remaining 3 tablespoons water as described on page 29. Stir until creamy and allow to cool to lukewarm; it should be thick enough to spread easily, but not stiff.

Using a butter knife, spread a thin layer of chocolate onto the bottom of each florentine and allow to cool until the chocolate has hardened. They may then be eaten immediately, or stored as described above.

INGREDIENTS FOR 8 TO 12 FLORENTINES

Generous ⅔ cup (140 g) granulated sugar
1 tablespoon (20 g) honey
7 tablespoons (105 ml) water
3 tablespoons (45 g) crème fraîche (p. 30) or heavy cream
⅓ cup (60 g) mixed diced candied orange peel and candied cherries
1 cup (100 g) slivered almonds
5¼ ounces (150 g) semisweet chocolate

PREPARATION TIME

About 40 minutes

Monsieur Robert's Ginger Florentines

FLORENTINS AU GINGEMBRE DE M. ROBERT

INGREDIENTS FOR ABOUT 8 TO 12 FLORENTINES

Generous ⅔ cup (140 g) granulated sugar
1 tablespoon (20 g) honey

7 tablespoons (105 ml) water
3 tablespoons (45 g) crème fraîche (p. 30) or heavy cream
⅓ cup (60 g) candied ginger, cut into ½-inch (1 cm) slivers
1 cup (100 g) slivered almonds

5¼ ounces (150 g) semisweet chocolate

PREPARATION TIME

About 40 minutes

T hese are for those who like candied ginger.

Procedure

Make the florentines exactly as described on page 105, but replace the candied orange peel and cherries with the candied ginger.

Coconut–Chocolate Fudge Cups

MINI-CROÛTES DE CHOCOLAT AU HOT FUDGE

INGREDIENTS FOR 12 TO 16 LITTLE CUPS

3½ ounces (100 g) semisweet chocolate
¼ cup (60 ml) water
5 tablespoons (75 g) butter, softened
1⅔ cups (125 g) dried grated coconut
Hot Fudge Sauce (p. 123)

PREPARATION TIME

The cups—30 to 35 minutes; the sauce—25 minutes

M ake these in advance, but keep them in a cool place, not in the refrigerator.

Procedure

Line smooth-sided petit-four molds, 1¼ to 1½ inches (3 to 4 cm) in diameter, with aluminum foil, leaving a border of foil extending over the edge.

In a saucepan, melt the chocolate with the water as described on page 29. Add the butter and stir until smooth and creamy. Remove from the heat and stir in the coconut. Using your fingers, press this mixture into the lined molds to form little cups; the coconut-chocolate layer should be thin and as even as possible. Place in the refrigerator to harden.

Make the Hot Fudge Sauce and allow it to cool to warm. Remove the molds from the refrigerator and fill them with the sauce. Set in a cool place to allow the sauce to stiffen to the consistency of a soft caramel.

When ready to serve, lift the little cups out of the molds by holding on to the edges of the aluminum foil, peel the foil off carefully, and serve on a serving platter.

Mini-Mont Blancs in Chocolate Cups

MINI-MONT-BLANC EN COUPELLES

These little cups are quite easy to prepare, but a pastry bag is essential for a perfect presentation. They can be made 2 to 3 hours in advance and kept in the refrigerator until ready to serve.

Procedure

To make the chocolate cups: Prepare and line smooth-sided petit-four molds, 1¼ to 1½ inches (3 to 4 cm) in diameter, exactly as described for Chocolate Cups Filled with Tangerine Jelly, page 100. Use the amount of chocolate indicated here.

To make the whipped cream: Follow the instructions on page 125, but eliminate the melted chocolate and use the quantities of cream, sugar, and vanilla sugar given here. Place the whipped cream in the refrigerator while the chocolate cups harden.

To make the chestnut puree: Place the canned chestnut puree, the sugar, milk, and rum in a mixing bowl and mix together well with a wooden spoon.

Remove the chocolate cups from the refrigerator, lift them out of the molds, and peel off the aluminum foil. Using a pastry bag equipped with a ⅜-inch (1 cm) nozzle, fill them with a mounded spiral of whipped cream. Then, using a second pastry bag equipped with the smallest nozzle you can find—1/32 to 1/16 inch (1 to 2 mm) —squeeze the chestnut puree on top of the whipped cream in a wiggly line. The puree should be piled up on itself, covering about ⅔ of the whipped cream but leaving a white border of cream around it. Place the finished mont blancs on a serving platter and keep in the refrigerator until ready to serve.

INGREDIENTS FOR 12 TO 16 LITTLE CUPS

The Chocolate Cups

9 ounces (250 g) semisweet chocolate

The Whipped Cream

1 cup (¼ l) heavy (whipping) cream
1 tablespoon granulated sugar
2 teaspoons vanilla sugar

The Chestnut Puree

⅞ cup (210 ml) canned chestnut puree
3 tablespoons (35 g) granulated sugar
3 tablespoons (50 ml) milk
1 teaspoon dark rum

PREPARATION TIME

About 1 hour

Chocolate Tile Cookies

TUILES AU CHOCOLAT

These cookies get their name from the fact that they look like the rounded tiles on the roofs of the houses in the south of France. Although they may be made in advance, they must be placed in a tightly closed cookie box as soon as they have cooled,

*1 tablespoon unsweetened cocoa
   powder*
¼ teaspoon ground cinnamon
6 tablespoons (60 g) flour
*3 tablespoons (30 g) chopped
   hazelnuts*
4 tablespoons (60 g) butter
3 tablespoons (50 g) corn syrup
⅓ cup (50 g) brown sugar

PREPARATION TIME

40 to 50 minutes

because the slightest humidity in the air makes them go stale in a very short time.

Procedure

Preheat the oven to 350°F (175°C).

Lightly butter a baking sheet.

In a mixing bowl, carefully mix together the cocoa, cinnamon, flour, and chopped hazelnuts.

Place the butter, corn syrup, and brown sugar in a saucepan. Bring to a boil over moderate heat, stirring constantly. As soon as the mixture is bubbling all over, stir in the flour-cocoa mixture little by little to form a uniform dough.

Using an ordinary tablespoon, drop little mounds of dough onto the baking sheet, leaving plenty of space between them because they will spread and flatten as they cook. Bake for 5 to 6 minutes, or until the edges look dry.

Remove the cookies from the oven, allow to cool, then lift them off the baking sheet (in this case they will be flat); or if you would like to give them their typical rounded shape, pull the baking sheet halfway out of the oven, but leave the oven on and the door wide open. One at a time, lift the cookies off the baking sheet with a spatula and set them upside down in your hand (protect your hand with a potholder or folded dish towel). Gently curve your toweled hand around the cookie to coax it into a "tile" shape (see photo following p. 104). Put the finished "tiles" on a cake rack to cool completely, then serve immediately, or place in a tightly closed cookie box until ready to serve.

*Variation: Chocolate Cones with Whipped Cream
and Grated Chocolate*

Make Whipped Cream with Grated Chocolate (p. 126).

Make the Chocolate Tile Cookies as described above, but instead of forming them into "tiles," form them into cones, pressing the edges together at the base (see photo following p. 104). Allow to cool completely on a cake rack.

When ready to serve, fill the cones with the whipped cream and serve on a serving platter.

LE CHOCOLAT

Chocolate Marzipan Cookies

MASSEPAINS AU CHOCOLAT

These little cookies are absolutely delicious with black coffee.

Procedure

Preheat the oven to 250°F (120°C).

Grate the chocolate and mix it with the sugar.

Beat the egg whites until firm, sprinkling in the chocolate-sugar mixture little by little as you beat. Fold in the slivered almonds.

Line a baking sheet with waxed paper. Butter lightly, then, using a teaspoon, drop little mounds of the batter onto the paper. Flatten them slightly.

Bake for 10 to 15 minutes, or until the surface looks dry; don't open the over door while the cookies are baking or they won't rise. Remove from the oven, allow to cool completely, then lift them off the waxed paper using a spatula.

INGREDIENTS FOR ABOUT 20 COOKIES

2¾ ounces (80 g) semisweet chocolate
¾ cup (150 g) granulated sugar
2 egg whites
¾ cup (60 g) slivered almonds

PREPARATION TIME

40 to 50 minutes

Creamy Chocolate Caramels

CARAMELS MOUS AU CHOCOLAT

The fresher these are, the better they are.

Procedure

Place all of the ingredients in a heavy-bottomed saucepan over low heat, stirring constantly, until the mixture comes to a boil. As you stir, scrape the sides of the saucepan to remove any sugar that sticks to them. Once the mixture is boiling, allow to simmer for a few minutes, until a little bit dropped from a spoon into a glass of cold water can be formed into a soft ball (240° to 244°F [115° to 118°C] on a candy thermometer).

Remove from the heat and pour into a frame formed by 4 oiled strips of wood set on an oiled marble slab or oiled baking sheet. Allow to cool almost completely, then cut into squares. Place on a cake rack to cool completely and stiffen, being careful that the candies do not touch one another.

INGREDIENTS FOR ABOUT 12 OUNCES (350 g) CARAMELS

¾ cup (150 g) granulated sugar
⅔ cup (75 g) unsweetened cocoa powder
6½ tablespoons (100 g) butter, cut into 6 pieces and allowed to soften

PREPARATION TIME

About 15 minutes

Cocoa Fudge with Pistachios

CACAO FUDGE AUX PISTACHES

INGREDIENTS FOR
ABOUT 2 POUNDS
(900 g) CANDY

*1½ cups (175 g) unsweetened
cocoa powder*
*2½ cups (500 g) granulated
sugar*
1 pinch salt
1 cup (¼ l) milk
6½ tablespoons (100 g) butter
1 teaspoon vanilla extract
⅔ cup (100 g) chopped pistachios

PREPARATION TIME

20 minutes

T hese candies should be eaten as soon as possible after being made.

Procedure

Place the cocoa, sugar, and salt in a saucepan. Little by little, stir in the milk, then add the butter and bring slowly to a boil, stirring constantly. When bubbling gently all over, cover the saucepan and cook for a few minutes more, or until a little of the mixture dropped from a teaspoon into a glass of cold water can be formed into a soft ball (240° to 244°F [115° to 118°C] on a candy thermometer).

Remove from the heat, allow to cool to warm, then add the vanilla and pistachios, stirring them in carefully.

Pour the mixture out onto an oiled marble slab or oiled baking sheet, into a square formed by placing 4 oiled strips of wood to hold the sides of the candy up. Allow to cool almost completely, then cut the candy into diamond shapes by cutting parallel lines from one side to the other, then kitty-corner. Remove the frame and place the candies on a cake rack to cool, being careful not to let them touch one another.

Pineapple Fudge

FUDGE À L'ANANAS

INGREDIENTS FOR 32
SQUARES OF FUDGE

*4¼ ounces (120 g) semisweet
chocolate*
6½ tablespoons (100 ml) milk
*1¼ cups (240 g) granulated
sugar*
1 pinch salt
3 tablespoons (40 g) butter
1 teaspoon vanilla extract
*2 tablespoons finely diced
candied pineapple*

Procedure

Butter 2 heatproof glass or porcelain dishes measuring about 4 by 6½ inches (10 × 16 cm).

In a saucepan, melt the chocolate with the milk as described on page 29. Stir until soft and creamy, then stir in the sugar and salt. Continue to heat, stirring, until the mixture begins to boil with craterlike bubbles. Stir in the butter, then remove from the heat and allow to cool. When barely lukewarm, stir in the vanilla extract, then beat vigorously with a wooden spoon until the fudge becomes dull; stir in the diced pineapple.

As soon as the pineapple has been mixed into the fudge, pour it into the buttered dishes; it should be about ½ to ¾ inch (1.5 to 2 cm) thick. With the tip of a knife, draw crisscross lines to form squares in the fudge. When the fudge is completely cold, cut out the squares along the lines, remove the candies from the dishes with a small flexible-blade metal spatula, and place in a tightly closed metal box until ready to serve.

PREPARATION TIME

20 to 30 minutes

Chocolate-Walnut Crunch

CROUSTILLANTS DE CHOCOLAT AUX NOIX

T hese crunchy little candies keep very well in a tightly closed metal box.

Procedure

In a saucepan, melt the chocolate with 1 tablespoon of the water as described on page 29. Stir until smooth and creamy; keep warm.

Place the sugar, butter, remaining 3 tablespoons water, and the salt in a second saucepan. Bring to a boil, stirring, then allow to cook at a gentle boil until a little of the mixture dropped into a glass of cold water can barely be formed into a soft ball (240°F [115°C] on a candy thermometer).

Stir in half the chopped walnuts, then pour the mixture out onto a lightly oiled marble slab or baking sheet in a thin, even layer. Allow to cool completely, then spread the melted chocolate over it and sprinkle with the remaining nuts.

When the chocolate is hard, break the candy into irregular pieces. Serve with coffee.

INGREDIENTS FOR 15 TO 20 CANDIES

$2^{3}/_{4}$ *ounces (75 g) semisweet chocolate*
4 tablespoons water
$^{2}/_{3}$ *cup (125 g) granulated sugar*
5 tablespoons (75 g) butter
1 pinch salt
$^{2}/_{3}$ *cup (60 g) coarsely chopped walnuts*

PREPARATION TIME

About 20 minutes

Honey Nougats from Saint-Étienne

CANOUGATS DE SAINT-ÉTIENNE

INGREDIENTS FOR ABOUT 20 CANDIES

5¼ ounces (150 g) semisweet chocolate
6½ tablespoons (100 ml) crème fraîche (p. 30) or heavy cream
⅔ cup (125 g) granulated sugar
2 tablespoons (30 g) butter
3 tablespoons honey

PREPARATION TIME

15 minutes

T|hese are soft chocolates with a taste of honey.

Procedure

Grate the chocolate and place it in a saucepan with the cream and sugar. Stir over high heat until a thick, smooth mixture is formed, then stir in the butter and finally the honey.

Remove from the heat and pour into a frame formed by 4 oiled wooden strips of wood on an oiled marble slab or oiled baking sheet. Allow to cool almost completely, then cut into lozenges or squares. Allow to cool completely on a cake rack, making sure they do not touch one another.

Chocolate Truffles

TRUFFES AU CHOCOLAT

INGREDIENTS FOR ABOUT 25 TRUFFLES

9 ounces (250 g) semisweet chocolate
¼ cup (60 ml) water
3 tablespoons (40 g) butter
¾ cup (200 ml) crème fraîche (p. 30) or heavy cream
2 tablespoons (20 g) confectioners' sugar
Unsweetened cocoa powder

PREPARATION TIME

15 minutes

T|hese are best when freshly made.

Procedure

In a saucepan, melt the chocolate with the water as described on page 29. Stir until smooth and creamy, then stir in the butter, piece by piece. Stir in the cream and confectioners' sugar; the finished mixture should be perfectly uniform in color and texture. Remove from the heat, allow to cool to room temperature, then place in the refrigerator to stiffen.

Spread some unsweetened cocoa powder on a soup plate.

Arrange about 25 little paper cases on a serving platter.

Remove the truffle mixture from the refrigerator and form it into little balls with your fingers. As each one is made, roll it in the cocoa, then place it in a little paper case. They are best served immediately, but if you must wait, return them to the refrigerator until ready to serve.

5

Chocolate Icings and Decorations

The object of decorating a cake is to make it attractive and to add a supplementary texture and flavor. In this chapter, you will find a few traditional recipes, easy to make, that can be transformed according to your imagination.

If you like, once the cake has been iced, you may continue to decorate it by squeezing an icing of another color onto it, or by stenciling stars, circles, and so forth onto it with confectioners' sugar. And of course there is an endless variety of sugar flowers, pearls, and so on that can be purchased. In my personal opinion, however, the simpler the cake, the better.

A well-made cake presented on a nice platter and decorated simply with a perfectly applied icing, or just sprinkled with cocoa powder, is always an elegant dessert. For those perfectionists who want to try their hand at something a little more special, though, I have included a few ideas for decoration at the end of the chapter.

HOW TO APPLY
A SMOOTH CHOCOLATE ICING

To make a cake easier to maneuver, cut a piece of thin cardboard the size of the cake and, when the cake is completely cooled, place it on the cardboard base, then set it on a pastry board or cake rack. (Some kitchenware and professional supply shops sell cardboard pastry bases in all kinds of sizes and shapes; they simply need to be trimmed slightly, and even this is not absolutely necessary.)

Make the Icing of Your Choice

When ready to use it, check the temperature. Icing should be lukewarm. Too hot, and it will be too runny to coat the cake correctly. Too cold and it will be too thick to spread evenly.

Icing the Cake

When the icing is the right consistency, pour it slowly onto the middle of the cake. With a wooden spatula, gently push it toward the edges of the cake so that it will run slowly down the sides. Smooth the icing where necessary with the spatula to even out the sides of the cake. When the entire cake is covered, run the tip of a knife all around the base to detach any puddles of icing that have piled up around it. Remove the excess icing from the pastry board and run the blade of a long, flexible-blade metal spatula under the cardboard base to prevent the icing from "gluing" it to the board or rack as it hardens. When the icing has set completely, slide the flexible-blade metal spatula under the cardboard base and transfer the cake to a serving platter.

Comment: If you want to ice only the top of the cake and leave the sides as they are, allow the icing to cool and thicken a bit more than if you were icing the whole cake. Slowly pour just enough icing for the top onto the center of the cake and coax it toward the edge with a wooden spatula. Use the flexible-blade metal spatula to form a little wall as you do so, to keep the icing from going over the edge.

Simple Chocolate Icing

GLAÇAGE SIMPLE

Procedure

Place the chocolate, water, and salt in a small saucepan. Melt over low heat, as described on page 29. Stir in the butter, piece by piece; the resulting icing should be smooth and shiny. Ice the top and sides of the cake as described on page 114.

Variations

1. Mocha Icing: Use 3 tablespoons (50 ml) water mixed with 1 tablespoon very strong coffee instead of the water. (This flavoring is extremely subtle.)
2. Orange-Chocolate Icing: Add ½ teaspoon curaçao or other orange-flavored liqueur to the water.

INGREDIENTS FOR ICING 1 CAKE THAT SERVES 6 TO 8

7 ounces (200 g) coating chocolate (p. 21) or semisweet chocolate
¼ cup (60 ml) water
1 pinch salt
5 tablespoons (75 g) butter, cut into 5 pieces and allowed to soften

PREPARATION TIME

10 minutes

Chocolate Mousse Icing

GLAÇAGE DE MOUSSE

Procedure

Place the chocolate and water in a small saucepan and melt as described on page 29. When the mixture is thick and creamy remove the pan from the heat and stir in the butter, piece by piece.

Add the egg yolks one at a time, stirring in each one completely before adding the next.

Place the egg whites in a large mixing bowl, add the salt, and beat until stiff. Pour the chocolate mixture onto the whites, and fold in carefully; the finished mixture should be of a uniform color.

Ice the top and sides of the cake with the mousse, then place it in the refrigerator so that the icing can set.

INGREDIENTS FOR ICING 1 CAKE THAT SERVES 6 TO 8

7 ounces (200 g) bittersweet chocolate
¼ cup (60 ml) water
3½ tablespoons (50 g) butter, cut into 4 pieces and allowed to soften
3 egg yolks
3 egg whites
1 pinch salt

Variations

1. With Coffee: Use ¼ cup (60 ml) strong coffee instead of water.
2. With Grand-Marnier: Once the mousse is made, fold in Grand-Marnier to taste (about 1 tablespoon, generally).
3. With Cinnamon: Mix ¼ teaspoon cinnamon into the water before adding it to the chocolate.

Chocolate Cream Icing

GLAÇAGE AU CHOCOLAT ET À LA CRÈME FRAÎCHE

INGREDIENTS FOR
ICING THE TOP OF 1
CAKE THAT SERVES
6 TO 8

*3½ ounces (100 g) semisweet
  chocolate*
2 tablespoons water
1 tablespoon granulated sugar
*6 tablespoons (90 ml) crème
  fraîche (p. 30) or heavy
  cream*

PREPARATION TIME

15 minutes

Procedure

Place the chocolate and water in a small saucepan and melt as described on page 29. When all the chocolate has softened, stir in the sugar; continue stirring until the mixture is very smooth.

Add the cream, stirring until the mixture is of a uniform color, then ice the top of the cake.

Buttery Chocolate Icing

GLAÇAGE AU BEURRE DE CHOCOLAT

INGREDIENTS FOR
ICING THE TOP OF 1
CAKE THAT SERVES
6 TO 8

*3½ ounces (100 g) bittersweet
  chocolate*
2 tablespoons water
*3½ tablespoons (50 g) butter,
  cut into 4 pieces and allowed
  to soften*

This is actually a sort of butter icing, so you may use the Chocolate Butter Cream on page 125 if you prefer. This one is simpler to make. Since it is very rich, I suggest that only the top of a cake be iced with it, in a very thin layer.

Procedure

Place the chocolate and water in a small saucepan and melt over low heat as described on page 29.

When the mixture is creamy, add the butter, piece by piece;

when finished, the icing should be the consistency of a light mayonnaise.

Remove from the heat and allow to cool to warm before icing the cake.

PREPARATION TIME

10 to 12 minutes

SOME OTHER IDEAS FOR DECORATING CAKES

Cocoa

Always use the best quality, unsweetened cocoa powder.

Place the cake on a cake rack.

Place the cocoa powder in a sifter or a fine sieve. Sprinkle the surface of the cake generously with the cocoa powder, in a thick layer.

With the aid of a large, flexible-blade metal spatula, slide the cake onto a serving platter.

Confectioners' Sugar

Follow the directions for using cocoa.

Cocoa Plus Confectioners' Sugar

This is for making two-toned decorations, black and white. The cake can be divided in half, quarters, or patterns can be cut out of cardboard: stars, circles, rings, and so forth. If you make cardboard patterns, be sure to tape a little handle on top so that the cardboard can be lifted straight off of the cake.

Place the cake on a cake rack. Sprinkle with cocoa as described above. Place the cardboard patterns in place. Sprinkle with confectioners' sugar. Lift off the cardboard patterns very carefully. With the aid of a large, flexible-blade metal spatula, slide the cake onto a serving platter.

Chocolate Shavings and Cigarettes

Chocolate shavings and cigarettes are used to decorate a cake that has just been iced or spread with a thin layer of jam. They are not very difficult to make, but one must be very careful when handling them in order not to break them.

I. SMALL CHOCOLATE SHAVINGS

Run a potato peeler along the edge of a large bar of chocolate, holding the bar over the cake so that the shavings will fall directly onto the soft icing or jam and stick to it.

2. LARGE CHOCOLATE SHAVINGS

Melt a large bar of semisweet chocolate in the top of a double boiler (do *not* add water to it). When the chocolate has completely melted, pour it onto a clean baking sheet, or marble or Formica slab, and spread it out into a wide, even layer. Allow it to set.

Before the chocolate has become completely hard, scrape the surface of it with the blade of a knife, tilted at a 45-degree angle, which has been dipped into hot water and wiped dry. Large shavings will be scraped off the surface of the chocolate in this way (the knife should be dipped into the hot water and dried whenever necessary). As they are made, place the shavings on a large platter (do not pile them up) and place in the refrigerator to harden. When hard, place them as you like on a cake that has just been iced or spread with a little jam.

3. CHOCOLATE CIGARETTES

Make large chocolate shavings exactly as described above. As each one is made, carefully roll it up into a cigarette shape; place the cigarettes on a platter to harden in the refrigerator as described for the large chocolate shavings. They can either be used to decorate a cake or be eaten on their own as an accompaniment to another dessert.

Almonds

Almonds can be bought either whole with their thin brown skins, whole and blanched, or in thick or thin slivers. If using almonds with their skins on, they should be peeled as follows: drop them into a pot of boiling water, leave them there for a couple of minutes, then drain. The skin will come off easily. Pat the peeled almonds dry in a dish towel.

Whether whole or slivered, the almonds should be browned before using. Spread them out on a baking sheet and place them under a low to moderate broiler. Watch carefully so that they don't burn, and turn them over to brown on all sides. Allow to cool.

The almonds may now be used as they are to decorate the surface of a cake, a cream dessert, ice cream, or a mousse. They may also be coarsely chopped and used in a cake filling, to decorate the sides of a cake, or to make a decorative border around the top of a cake.

Walnuts

Walnut meats are sold commercially; if at all possible, buy ones that have been picked that year.

They can be used as is to decorate the surface of a cake or coarsely chopped to decorate the sides of a cake. They add a wonderful flavor when used in this way.

6

Sauces and Fillings

These are basic recipes for sauces and fillings. Although the fillings are used here to garnish or accompany chocolate desserts and cakes, they are not limited to that. Try them with other desserts you already make—you may just find that they add a little something that makes a familiar dessert special. After all, chocolate goes with just about everything.

Hot Chocolate Sauce

SAUCE CHAUDE AU CHOCOLAT

INGREDIENTS FOR
1⅔ CUPS (375 ML)
SAUCE

*6 ounces (170 g) bittersweet
chocolate*
1 cup (240 ml) water
*3½ tablespoons (50 g) butter,
cut into 4 pieces and allowed
to soften*

PREPARATION TIME

10 to 12 minutes

Theoretically, this sauce should be made at the last minute, since it is served hot. But in fact, it can be kept warm over very low heat or even made well in advance and reheated in a double boiler.

Procedure

Place the chocolate and ¼ cup (60 ml) of the water in a small saucepan; when the chocolate begins to soften, stir to make a smooth cream.

Piece by piece, stir in the butter, then stir in the rest of the water. Bring to a boil, stirring—the sauce will thicken considerably.

Pour into a sauceboat and serve immediately.

Variations

1. With Coffee: Melt the chocolate with 2 tablespoons strong coffee and 2 tablespoons water, instead of ¼ cup (60 ml) water. Continue as described above.

2. With Whiskey: Make the sauce as described, then, just before serving, stir in 1 to 2 teaspoons whiskey.

Hot Fudge Sauce (page 123)

Whipped Cream with Grated Chocolate (page 126)

Cold Drinks (pages 129–131)

Hot Drinks (pages 132–134)

Orange-Flavored Chocolate Sauce

SAUCE DE CHOCOLAT À L'ORANGE

T his sauce should be made at the last minute.

Procedure

Parboil the orange zests for 1 minute in boiling water, drain, and dry in a clean cloth.

Place the chocolate in the top of a double boiler, melt as described on page 29, then stir in the other ingredients. Continue to stir until the sauce is thick and creamy.

Pour into a sauceboat and serve immediately.

INGREDIENTS FOR ABOUT 1 CUP (250 ML) SAUCE

2 tablespoons thinly cut (julienne strips) orange zest
7 ounces (200 g) semisweet chocolate
¼ cup (60 ml) curaçao or other orange-flavored liqueur
3 tablespoons (30 g) confectioners' sugar
¼ cup (60 ml) water

PREPARATION TIME

20 minutes

Honey-Flavored Chocolate Sauce

SAUCE DE CHOCOLAT AU MIEL

T his sauce can be served either hot or cold and is the perfect accompaniment to numerous cakes and desserts.

Procedure

Place the chocolate and honey in a small saucepan over low heat. When the chocolate has begun to melt, shake the saucepan in a circular motion to make the chocolate and honey swirl around the sides and mix together.

In a small mixing bowl, stir the cornstarch into a spoonful of the cream. When it has completely dissolved, stir in the rest of the cream.

Whisk the cream and cornstarch mixture into the chocolate and bring slowly to a boil. When the sauce is thick and creamy, remove from the heat.

Serve either hot or cold.

INGREDIENTS FOR ABOUT 1¾ CUPS (420 ML) SAUCE

8 ounces (225 g) semisweet chocolate, broken into pieces
5 tablespoons (100 g) honey (preferably liquid)
1 teaspoon cornstarch
Generous ¾ cup (200 ml) heavy cream

PREPARATION TIME

20 to 22 minutes

Rum-Coffee Fudge Sauce

FUDGE DE CHOCOLAT AU RHUM ET AU CAFÉ

INGREDIENTS FOR ABOUT 2 CUPS (500 ML) SAUCE

1 stick plus 1 tablespoon (125 g) butter, softened
1 cup plus 2 tablespoons (220 g) granulated sugar
5 tablespoons (50 g) unsweetened cocoa powder
2 tablespoons dark rum
Generous ¾ cup (200 ml) heavy cream
1 teaspoon instant coffee
1 pinch salt

PREPARATION TIME

20 minutes

This sauce may be served either hot, warm, or cold. It will keep for a week in the refrigerator and can be reheated in a double boiler.

Procedure

In a heavy-bottomed saucepan, melt the butter over low heat. Stir in the sugar, cocoa powder, rum, and cream, and bring slowly to a boil.

Stir in the instant coffee and salt and bring back to a boil. Allow to boil gently for 7 to 10 minutes, then remove from the heat.

Serve hot, warm, or cold.

Chocolate Sabayon

SABAYON DE CHOCOLAT

INGREDIENTS FOR 4 SERVINGS

3½ ounces (100 g) semisweet chocolate
2 tablespoons water
1 pinch salt
4 egg yolks
¼ cup (50 g) granulated sugar

PREPARATION TIME

15 to 20 minutes

This sauce should be served at room temperature; it is made at the last minute. It is an excellent accompaniment to cakes, desserts, and ice creams.

Procedure

Place the chocolate, water, and salt in a small saucepan and melt over low heat as described on page 29. When smooth and creamy, cover the pan and remove from the heat.

In a thick-bottomed saucepan, beat the egg yolks and sugar together until the mixture forms a ribbon. Place over very low heat (or use a double boiler) and heat, whisking constantly, until thick and foamy.

Whisk in the chocolate, a generous tablespoonful at a time, then remove from the heat. The sauce is ready; pour into a sauceboat and serve immediately.

Hot Fudge Sauce

HOT FUDGE SAUCE

This is a very rich sauce with an almost caramel taste, delicious with ice cream, desserts, and cakes. Served warm or hot, it is best to make it at the last minute, but it can be made in advance and reheated over low heat.

Procedure

Mix the cocoa powder and 3 tablespoons of the melted butter together in a small mixing bowl.

Place the remaining butter in a small saucepan over low heat and stir in the cocoa-butter mixture, sugar, and salt. The mixture should become very grainy. Add the water, little by little, stirring constantly over low heat. The sauce should become smooth but quite liquid.

Bring to a boil, stirring. Allow to simmer for 15 minutes, stirring from time to time. When the sauce is smooth and creamy, remove from the heat and allow to cool slightly before serving.

INGREDIENTS FOR 6 TO 8 SERVINGS

½ cup (75 g) unsweetened cocoa powder
7 tablespoons (105 g) butter, melted
1 cup (200 g) granulated sugar
1 pinch salt
½ cup (120 ml) water

PREPARATION TIME

35 minutes

Chocolate Custard Sauce

CRÈME ANGLAISE AU CHOCOLAT

This sauce must be made well in advance so that it has time to cool. It is not a bad idea to make it a day ahead of time.

Procedure

Bring the milk to a boil and whisk in the cocoa powder. Remove from the heat.

In a mixing bowl, beat the egg yolks and sugar together until creamy, then whisk in the hot milk, little by little. Pour back into the saucepan and cook, stirring constantly over low heat until the sauce lightly coats the spoon. Test to see if it is done by drawing a line in the cream on the spoon with your finger; if it is ready, the top edge of the line will hold its shape. *Do not allow to boil*, or the sauce will fall apart.

Remove the sauce from the heat and strain it into a bowl. Beat it gently for 5 to 10 minutes as it cools, to make it lighter. When cool, place it in the refrigerator until ready to use.

INGREDIENTS FOR 4¼ CUPS (1 L) SAUCE, SERVING 8

1 quart (950 ml) milk
Generous 3 tablespoons (45 g) unsweetened cocoa powder
7 egg yolks
⅓ cup (70 g) granulated sugar

PREPARATION TIME

15 to 20 minutes

To serve, stir gently, then pour into a sauceboat or serving dish, depending on the dessert. Serve cold.

Variations

1. Vanilla Custard Sauce: Use 1 vanilla bean, cut in half length-wise, instead of the cocoa powder. Place it in the cold milk, bring to a boil, and whisk. Make the sauce exactly as described, leaving the vanilla bean in the whole time until you strain the sauce into the bowl to cool.

2. Coffee Custard Sauce: Make exactly like Chocolate Custard Sauce, but use instant coffee instead of cocoa powder.

Chocolate-Caramel Custard Sauce

CRÈME ANGLAISE AU CHOCOLAT CARAMÉLISÉ

INGREDIENTS FOR
4¼ CUPS (1 L) SAUCE,
TO SERVE 8

3¼ cups (¾ l) milk
½ cup (100 g) granulated sugar
3 tablespoons (50 ml) water
4¼ ounces (125 g) semisweet
  chocolate
6 egg yolks

PREPARATION TIME

30 to 35 minutes

T his sauce can be made up to a day in advance and kept in the refrigerator. It is used with cakes and desserts.

Procedure

Heat the milk in a small saucepan until warm.

In a second, heavy-bottomed saucepan, place the sugar and water over moderate heat and stir gently until the sugar has dissolved. Stop stirring and allow the sugar to cook until it begins to change color, then swirl the saucepan so that the sugar colors evenly. When it is a rich golden caramel color, remove from the heat.

Continue swirling the saucepan until the bubbles die down, then stir in the warm milk, ⅓ at a time (stand back when you add the first ⅓ because it will splatter). Scrape the bottom of the saucepan as you add the milk to dissolve the caramel stuck to it—once all the milk has been added, it may take 5 to 10 minutes' more stirring for all the hard pieces to melt.

In the first saucepan, place the chocolate and 3 tablespoons of the caramelized milk. Melt over low heat, stirring, then stir in the rest of the milk.

In a mixing bowl, beat the egg yolks lightly, then whisk in the flavored milk. Pour back into the saucepan and cook over low heat, stirring constantly, until the sauce lightly coats the spoon and a horizontal line drawn in it with your finger holds its shape. *Do not allow to boil.*

Remove from the heat and strain the sauce into a bowl. Allow to cool, whisking from time to time to make it lighter. Chill before serving.

Chocolate Butter Cream

CRÈME AU BEURRE AU CHOCOLAT

This is the classic butter cream filling used in layer cakes. I'm giving this recipe because a lot of people like it, but I personally prefer lighter, less rich cake fillings. It is best made at the last minute. Since it spoils quickly, it is advisable to place a cake using it in the refrigerator until ready to serve.

Procedure

In a mixing bowl, beat the egg yolks and sugar until pale in color and creamy. With a wooden spoon, beat in the butter, piece by piece, then stir in the cocoa powder.

When the cocoa has been mixed in, beat the butter cream vigorously with a wooden spoon to make it very light and creamy in texture.

If not using immediately, keep at room temperature, covered with aluminum foil, for up to an hour.

Note: Leftover butter cream may be kept in the refrigerator for up to two days. Before using, remove from the refrigerator and let sit for an hour to soften, then stir to make smooth and spread. Ed.

INGREDIENTS FOR ABOUT 2 CUPS (500 ML) BUTTER CREAM

6 egg yolks
¾ cup (150 g) granulated sugar
2¼ sticks (250 g) butter, cut into 15 pieces and allowed to soften
5 tablespoons (50 g) unsweetened cocoa powder

PREPARATION TIME

15 to 20 minutes

Whipped Cream with Melted Chocolate

CRÈME CHANTILLY AU CHOCOLAT FONDU

The whipped cream may be made several hours in advance and kept cold in the refrigerator. The melted chocolate should be added just before serving.

This cream can be used to accompany, decorate, or garnish cakes and desserts.

Procedure

Place the mixing bowl the cream is to be whipped in in the refrigerator for 10 to 15 minutes. Both the bowl and the cream must be very cold.

Place the cream and both kinds of sugar in the mixing bowl. Whisk gently at first, until the cream has increased in volume, then beat energetically until it forms soft peaks. Do not beat too much, however, or the cream will turn to butter. Place in the refrigerator until ready to use.

Place the chocolate and water in a small saucepan over low heat. Melt the chocolate as described on page 29. When smooth and creamy, allow to cool.

Remove the whipped cream from the refrigerator; if any water has separated out, whisk it lightly to beat the water back into it. Fold the melted chocolate into the cream.

When the cream is of a uniform color, it is ready to use.

Note: To make vanilla sugar, cut a vanilla bean in half lengthwise and scrape the pulp out onto 1¹/₃ cups (150 g) lump sugar that has been placed in a heavy-duty blender or food processor. Blend or process until the sugar has been reduced to a powder, then store in a jar away from the light.

Whipped Cream with Grated Chocolate

CRÈME FOUETTÉE AU CHOCOLAT RÂPÉ

T his cream is made at the last minute; it is a nice, light accompaniment for very rich cakes.

Procedure

Place the mixing bowl to be used for whipping the cream in the refrigerator. Both the bowl and the cream should be very cold.

Place the cream and both kinds of sugar in the mixing bowl and beat gently until the cream has increased in volume, then beat vigorously until it forms soft peaks. Do not beat too much, or the cream will turn to butter.

Sprinkle the grated chocolate over the surface of the cream and fold it in gently.

Transfer the cream to a serving bowl and serve.

7

Drinks

BASIC PREPARATIONS

COLD DRINKS

HOT DRINKS

I n the beginning, chocolate was consumed as a drink. Since its discovery, it has been drunk in many ways, in many forms. In this chapter you will find beverages for all seasons, easy to make, hot and cold, with or without alcohol, which will help you pass a pleasant moment, even on an ordinary day.

Chocolate Syrup

SIROP DE CHOCOLAT

INGREDIENTS FOR ABOUT 2 CUPS (½ L) SYRUP

5¼ ounces (150 g) semisweet
   chocolate
1 pinch salt
1 cup (¼ l) water, heated
1¼ cups (240 g) granulated
   sugar
1 teaspoon vanilla extract

PREPARATION TIME

About 15 minutes

Procedure

Place the chocolate, salt, and 3 tablespoons of the water in a saucepan and melt as described on page 29. Stir until smooth, then stir in the rest of the water and the sugar.

   Bring to a boil, stirring constantly, then allow to boil gently for 5 minutes. Remove from the heat, allow to cool, then stir in the vanilla extract. Pour into a jar or bottle, seal tightly, and store in the refrigerator until ready to use.

Cocoa Syrup

SIROP DE CACAO

INGREDIENTS FOR ABOUT 2¼ CUPS (½ L) SYRUP

1½ cups (180 g) unsweetened
   cocoa powder
1½ cups (300 g) granulated
   sugar
1 pinch salt
1 cup (¼ l) water
1 teaspoon vanilla extract

PREPARATION TIME

About 15 minutes

Procedure

In a saucepan, stir the cocoa, sugar, and salt together, then, little by little, stir in the water. Bring to a boil over low heat, stirring constantly, then allow to boil gently for 5 minutes.

   Remove from the heat, allow to cool, then stir in the vanilla extract. Pour into a glass jar or bottle, seal tightly, and store in the refrigerator until ready to use.

Cream of Cocoa

CRÈME DE CACAO

Procedure

Place the sugar and water in a saucepan and bring to a boil, stirring until the sugar has dissolved. Boil for about 20 minutes, or until the syrup has reduced by half, scraping any sugar that collects on the sides of the saucepan back into the boiling syrup with a wooden spoon.

While the syrup is cooking, melt the chocolate with the water in a second saucepan, as described on page 29.

As soon as the syrup is ready, pour it slowly onto the melted chocolate, whisking vigorously to form a smooth, creamy mixture (if the mixture is at all grainy, pour it into a blender and blend until smooth; pour back into the saucepan to cool).

Allow the cream to cool for about 30 minutes, stirring occasionally, then stir in the vodka little by little and flavor with the vanilla extract. Pour into a bottle, seal tightly, and store in a kitchen cabinet until ready to use.

INGREDIENTS FOR ABOUT 2¾ CUPS (650 ML)

1¼ cups (240 g) granulated sugar
Scant 1⅔ cups (375 ml) water (for the syrup)
1½ ounces (40 g) bittersweet chocolate
1 tablespoon water (for the chocolate)
¾ cup (175 ml) vodka
½ teaspoon vanilla extract

PREPARATION TIME

About 30 minutes

Coffee Frappé with Chocolate Ice Cream

FRAPPÉ DE CAFÉ À LA GLACE AU CHOCOLAT

Everything is mixed just before serving, but you must be sure to prepare the ingredients well ahead of time so that they will be the correct temperature.

Procedure

Make the coffee well ahead of time and chill in the refrigerator until ready to serve.

About 30 minutes before serving, move the ice cream from the freezer to the refrigerator so that it won't be too hard.

In a mixing bowl, whisk together the milk, coffee, chocolate syrup, and rum. Divide among 4 large glasses, and place a large scoop of ice cream in each one.

Sprinkle with grated chocolate and serve with straws. This is delicious, especially when drunk slowly, stirring with the straw from time to time to mix all the flavors together.

INGREDIENTS FOR 4 LARGE GLASSES

Scant 1⅔ cups (375 ml) very strong coffee, chilled
4 large scoops Chocolate Ice Cream (p.40)
Scant 1⅔ cups (375 ml) milk, chilled
6½ tablespoons (100 ml) Chocolate Syrup (p. 128)
1 tablespoon rum
Grated chocolate

PREPARATION TIME

10 to 15 minutes

Chocolate-Cinnamon Milkshake

CHOCOLAT GLACÉ À LA CANELLE

INGREDIENTS FOR 2 LARGE GLASSES

3 cups (700 ml) milk, very well chilled

6 tablespoons (90 ml) Cocoa Syrup (p. 128)

4 scoops Chocolate Ice Cream (p. 40)

Ground cinnamon

PREPARATION TIME

5 minutes

T his is very quick to make; the ice cream and milk should be very cold.

Procedure

Place all of the ingredients except the cinnamon in a blender and blend on medium speed until smooth and foamy.

Pour into 2 large glasses and sprinkle with cinnamon. Serve with straws.

Chocolate Ice Cream Soda

ICE CREAM SODA DE CHOCOLAT

INGREDIENTS FOR 2 LARGE GLASSES

¼ cup (60 ml) heavy (whipping) cream, very well chilled

1 teaspoon vanilla sugar (see note to Whipped Cream with Melted Chocolate, p. 125)

6½ tablespoons (100 ml) milk, chilled

¼ cup (60 ml) Chocolate Syrup (p. 128)

2 scoops vanilla ice cream

2 scoops Chocolate Ice Cream (p. 40)

½ small bottle soda water, chilled

PREPARATION TIME

10 to 15 minutes

Procedure

Whip the cream and vanilla sugar together in a chilled bowl until it forms soft peaks. Keep in the refrigerator.

Mix the milk and Chocolate Syrup together and divide the mixture between 2 large glasses. Place a scoop of vanilla ice cream in each glass and more or less break it up and mix it into the chocolate milk. Place a scoop of Chocolate Ice Cream carefully on top, then fill the glass with soda water. Stir gently to mix it with the vanilla-chocolate mixture without hurting the scoop of Chocolate Ice Cream. Top with whipped cream and serve with a straw.

Cocoa-Cognac Cocktail

CACAO-COGNAC

T his cocktail is made in a shaker.

Procedure

To frost the glasses: Set one glass at a time upside down in the syrup, then in the cocoa, to make a thin cocoa border all around the edge. Hold the glass upside down for a few seconds after dipping it in the cocoa to let any excess fall off and to allow the cocoa stuck to the glass to dry a little. Set it right side up to dry completely while frosting the other glasses and making the cocktail.

To make the cocktail: Place all the ingredients in a cocktail shaker and shake vigorously to obtain a uniform foamy mixture. Pour carefully into the glasses, being careful not to touch the cocoa frosting, and serve. Don't use straws, because half the pleasure is tasting the cocoa at the same time as the drink.

INGREDIENTS FOR
TWO 4-OUNCE
COCKTAIL GLASSES

To Frost the Glasses

A saucerful of sugar syrup
*A saucerful of unsweetened
 cocoa powder*

The Cocktail

3 ounces (90 ml) milk
3 ounces (90 ml) Cognac
*1 teaspoon unsweetened cocoa
 powder*
2 teaspoons granulated sugar
1 egg yolk
A few ice cubes

PREPARATION TIME

15 minutes

Coffee-Chocolate Granisado

GRANISADO DE CAFÉ AU CHOCOLAT

T his is a light, refreshing drink that can be made at the last minute if the coffee is made ahead of time.

Procedure

Make the coffee, allow to cool, and chill in the refrigerator until ready to use.

When ready to serve, mix the coffee and the chocolate syrup. Fill 2 large glasses with crushed ice, pour the coffee-chocolate mixture over it, and serve with straws.

INGREDIENTS FOR 2
LARGE GLASSES

*½ cup (120 ml) very strong
 coffee, chilled*
*4 tablespoons Chocolate Syrup
 (p. 128)*
Crushed ice

PREPARATION TIME

1 to 2 minutes

Old-Fashioned Bavarian Cream

BAVAROISE À L'ANCIENNE

INGREDIENTS FOR 4 SERVINGS

4¼ ounces (120 g) semisweet
    chocolate
2 cups (½ l) milk
3 egg yolks
½ cup (120 ml) sugar syrup
1 teaspoon vanilla extract

PREPARATION TIME

About 15 minutes

T his is an old recipe. It's made at the last minute and served hot in tumblers.

Procedure

Melt the chocolate with 3 tablespoons of the milk as described on page 29. Stir until smooth, then stir in the rest of the milk. Keep warm.

In a mixing bowl, beat the egg yolks, syrup, and vanilla extract until the mixture lightens in color and becomes creamy. Whisk in the warm chocolate milk.

Pour back into the saucepan the chocolate milk was made in and heat over low heat, whisking constantly until the mixture has thickened slightly and become foamy. *Do not allow to boil.* Pour into tumblers and serve immediately.

Grandma's Hot Chocolate

CHOCOLAT DE GRAND-MÈRE

INGREDIENTS FOR 1 SERVING

1¼ ounces (35 g) semisweet
    chocolate
1 to 2 grains coarse salt
½ cup (120 ml) milk

PREPARATION TIME

6 to 7 minutes

T his hot chocolate is delicious, especially if you make it the night before and reheat it in the morning.

Procedure

Place the chocolate, grains of salt, and 1 tablespoon of the milk in a saucepan. Melt as described on page 29, stir until smooth, then stir in the rest of the milk. Bring to a boil and allow to simmer for 2 to 3 minutes, then serve, or allow to cool and bring just to a boil the next morning.

Chocolate Cappuccino

CAPPUCCINO DE CHOCOLAT

T his is a variation on the more familiar coffee cappuccino.

Procedure

Place the chocolate, salt, and 3 tablespoons of the water in a saucepan; melt as described on page 29. Stir until smooth, then add the sugar, and stir until it has melted.

Add the remaining water little by little, bring to a boil, and allow to boil slowly for a few minutes while you whip the cream.

Place the cold cream in a chilled mixing bowl with the vanilla sugar and beat until it forms soft peaks. Pour the hot chocolate into the cups, spoon a dollop of cream on top of each one, and serve immediately.

INGREDIENTS FOR 4 SERVINGS

5¼ ounces (150 g) semisweet chocolate

1 pinch salt

2 cups plus 3 tablespoons (525 ml) water

4 teaspoons granulated sugar

¼ cup (60 ml) heavy (whipping) cream, well chilled

¾ teaspoon vanilla sugar (see note to Whipped Cream with Melted Chocolate, p. 125)

PREPARATION TIME

10 to 15 minutes

Hot Chocolate with Rum and Coffee

CHOCOLAT CHAUD PARFUMÉ AU RHUM ET AU CAFÉ

T his is a wonderful drink to warm you up on a cold day.

Procedure

In a saucepan, melt the chocolate in the water as described on page 29. Stir until smooth; add the sugar and bring to a boil, stirring. Allow the mixture to bubble gently for 5 minutes, stirring constantly and scraping the bottom of the pan to keep the mixture from sticking.

Little by little, stir in the coffee, the rum, and the cream. Continue heating until boiling, then remove immediately from the heat and serve.

INGREDIENTS FOR 6 SERVINGS

6 ounces (170 g) semisweet chocolate

¼ cup (60 ml) water

5 tablespoons (60 g) granulated sugar

1 cup strong black coffee

1 tablespoon dark rum

1⅔ cups (400 ml) heavy cream

PREPARATION TIME

About 20 minutes

DRINKS

Old-Fashioned Hot Chocolate

CHOCOLAT À L'EAU

INGREDIENTS FOR 4
SERVINGS

*5 ounces (140 g) semisweet
  chocolate, grated*
4 cups (950 ml) water

PREPARATION TIME

About 15 minutes

For ages chocolate was made with water instead of milk and without any additional sugar in it. It was traditionally beaten until very foamy and served in a special chocolate pot.

Procedure

Place the chocolate in a saucepar with 3 tablespoons of the water and melt as described on page 29. Stir until smooth, then add the rest of the water little by little. Bring to a boil, stirring, then lower the heat and allow to simmer for 5 minutes, whisking constantly to make the chocolate foamy. Pour into cups or, if you have one, into an old-fashioned chocolate pot with a wooden swizzle, and serve.

Mexican-Style Hot Chocolate

CHOCOLAT MEXICAIN

INGREDIENTS FOR 4
SERVINGS

*5¼ ounces (150 g) semisweet
  chocolate, grated*
1½ cups (350 ml) milk
1 pinch salt
¾ cup (175 ml) heavy cream
2 tablespoons granulated sugar
*1 tablespoon ground cinnamon
  (or less, to taste)*
1 pinch ground cloves
1 whole egg
1 teaspoon vanilla extract

PREPARATION TIME

15 to 20 minutes

This is a delicious aromatic chocolate that can be started in advance and finished just before serving.

Procedure

Place the chocolate in a saucepan with 3 tablespoons of the milk and the salt. Melt as described on page 29. Stir until smooth, then add the rest of the milk, the cream, sugar, and spices. Bring to a boil, whisking, then lower the heat and allow to simmer for 5 minutes. At this point, you can set the chocolate aside, then reheat it and continue the recipe just before serving.

In a mixing bowl, beat the egg and vanilla extract together until foamy. Heat the chocolate; when very hot, but not boiling, whisk a tablespoonful of it into the egg. Whisk a second tablespoonful of chocolate into the egg, then pour the egg mixture into the saucepan of hot chocolate. Continue heating over low heat, without allowing to boil, whisking with an electric mixer or a hand whisk to make the chocolate very foamy (about five minutes). Serve immediately in large cups.

8

Main Dishes Using Chocolate

Although the idea of putting chocolate in a dish with meat or fish is shocking to many, traditional Spanish and Mexican recipes use it in its purest form, unsweetened, as a flavoring in many dishes. For the most part, they are highly seasoned dishes that cook very slowly for a long time.

In this chapter you will find a few of these traditional dishes, as well as some new ideas that are well worth a try.

Roast Duck with Chocolate

CANARD RÔTI AU CHOCOLAT

INGREDIENTS FOR 4 TO 5 SERVINGS

1 carrot, thinly sliced
2 medium onions, thinly sliced
2 stalks celery, thinly sliced
1 sprig thyme or ¼ teaspoon thyme leaves
1 bay leaf
One 3-pound 5-ounce (1.5 kg) duck, ready for roasting
Salt and pepper
¾ cup (200 ml) crème fraîche (p. 30) or heavy cream
1 tablespoon unsweetened cocoa powder
¼ cup (60 ml) dry white wine
1 cup (¼ l) chicken stock

PREPARATION TIME

1 hour 15 minutes to 1 hour 20 minutes

Procedure

Preheat the oven to 425°F (225°C).

Lightly butter a roasting pan, cover the bottom with the sliced vegetables, and add the thyme and bay leaf. Set the duck on top of these seasonings and sprinkle with salt and pepper. Heat on top of the stove until the vegetables begin to make a sizzling noise, then place in the oven.

After 30 minutes, remove the duck from the oven, set it on a plate, and pour the vegetables into a large strainer over a bowl. Place the duck back in the roasting pan to finish cooking for another 15 to 20 minutes, or until the juice that comes out of the center of a leg is pink (not dark red) when a trussing needle is inserted into it. While the duck finishes cooking, press on the vegetables to extract any fat or juices they contain. Baste the duck with these juices once or twice as it cooks.

Mix the cream and cocoa powder together in a bowl and reserve.

When the duck has finished cooking, remove it from the oven, place it on a serving platter, and cover with aluminum foil. Lower the oven to 300°F (150°C), place the duck inside, but leave the door ajar.

Discard all but about a tablespoon of fat from the roasting pan. Set the pan over high heat on top of the stove, add the white wine to the pan juices, and bring to a fast boil, scraping the bottom of the pan to detach any juices stuck to it. Boil until the pan is almost dry, then add the stock and cocoa-cream mixture. Continue boiling rapidly until reduced by half, then correct for seasoning. Pour into a sauceboat and serve with the duck.

Mexican-Style Turkey or Mole Poblano de Guajolote

DINDE À LA MEXICAINE OU MOLE POBLANO DE GUAJOLOTE

This is a traditional, spicy Mexican dish.

Procedure

Place the pieces of turkey in a large pot, add the onion, celery, peppercorns, and enough water to cover. Bring to a boil, skim off any foam that surfaces, lower the heat, and simmer for 2 hours.

After the turkey has cooked for about 1 hour, grind the chili peppers and bell peppers to a puree in a heavy-duty blender or food processor. Place in a bowl, moisten with ½ cup (120 ml) of the turkey stock and allow to sit for 30 minutes. At the end of that time, strain the mixture through a fine sieve, pressing with a wooden spoon to extract as much liquid and pulp as possible. Reserve.

In a mixing bowl, knead the corn flour with enough water to make a firm, stiff dough. With your hands, form it into 2 balls, then flatten each into a very thin pancake, or tortilla. Lightly oil a frying pan and cook the tortillas over moderate heat until brown on one side; turn over and brown on the other side, then remove from the pan and allow to cool completely. Crumble the tortillas into tiny pieces.

Peel the tomatoes by dropping them into boiling water for 10 to 15 seconds, draining, and cooling under running water; the skins will peel off easily. Cut each tomato in half crosswise, gently squeeze out the seeds, then chop coarsely. Reserve.

Wrap the peanuts in a dish towel and crush them as fine as possible by rolling a bottle over the peanuts repeatedly while you lean your weight upon it.

Mix the tortilla flakes, tomatoes, peanuts, onion, and garlic in a bowl with salt and pepper. In a saucepan, melt 2 tablespoons of the lard, add the mixture, bring to a boil, then lower the heat and allow to simmer for 5 minutes, stirring occasionally. In a bowl, mix the cocoa powder with the reserved pepper-stock mixture, pour this into the saucepan, cover, and continue to simmer slowly for 35 to 40 minutes.

When the turkey has finished cooking, remove it from the pot, then carefully dry each piece with a clean cloth. Reserve until the sauce has finished cooking.

INGREDIENTS FOR 8 SERVINGS

The Turkey

1 small, 5½- to 6½-pound (2.5 to 3 kg) turkey, cut into 8 pieces
1 onion, stuck with 2 cloves
3 stalks celery
10 peppercorns
Water to cover

The Sauce

3 chili peppers, preferably fresh, seeded, and cut into 1-inch (2.5 cm) pieces
3 bell peppers, seeded and cut into 1½-inch (4 cm) squares
¾ cup (100 g) corn flour
1 pinch salt
Oil or lard (for cooking tortillas)
4 medium tomatoes
Scant ½ cup (60 g) unsalted, shelled peanuts
1 onion, finely chopped
3 cloves garlic, finely chopped
Salt and pepper
3 tablespoons lard (for cooking sauce and browning turkey)
Generous ½ cup (70 g) unsweetened cocoa powder

PREPARATION TIME

The turkey—2 hours; the elements for the sauce—1 hour; cooking the sauce and finishing —45 to 50 minutes

When the sauce is done, melt the remaining 1 tablespoon of the lard in a large *sauteuse* or low-sided pot. When the lard is almost smoking, add the pieces of turkey and brown on all sides over moderately high heat. Add the sauce and allow to cook slowly together for 8 to 10 minutes, then serve, either in the pot, or in a heated serving dish.

Castilian-Style Pork

ÉCHINE DE PORC À LA CASTILLANE

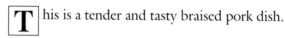

INGREDIENTS FOR 4 SERVINGS

2 tablespoons cooking oil
2 onions, coarsely chopped
2 pounds (900 g) fresh pork butt (Boston shoulder), in 1 piece
¼ cup (60 ml) dry white wine
½ cup (120 ml) stock or water
1 clove garlic, crushed
Salt and pepper
1 pinch nutmeg
¾ cup (60 g) slivered almonds
1 tablespoon unsweetened cocoa powder

PREPARATION TIME

50 to 55 minutes

T his is a tender and tasty braised pork dish.

Procedure

Heat the oil in a pot just large enough to hold the pork comfortably. Add the onions and cook over low heat until transparent and golden brown. Lift out the onions with a skimmer or slotted spoon and reserve on a plate.

Place the pork in the pot and brown on all sides over moderate heat, then put the onions back into the pot, add the wine and stock or water, garlic, salt, pepper, and nutmeg. Bring just to a boil, then lower the heat, cover the pot, and simmer for 40 to 45 minutes.

While the pork is cooking, brown the almonds as described on page 118. Heat a serving platter with enough of an indentation to hold the sauce.

When the meat is cooked and tender, lift it out of the pot and keep it warm on the serving platter. Raise the heat under the pot and bring the sauce to a rapid boil, then sprinkle in the cocoa powder, stirring. When all of the cocoa is mixed in, lower the heat and allow to simmer for 5 minutes, then pour the sauce over the meat, sprinkle with the browned almonds, and serve.

Alain Senderens's Duck with Orange-Chocolate Sauce

CANARD AU CHOCOLAT D'ALAIN SENDERENS

T he great, three-star chef Alain Senderens invented this recipe especially for this book.

Procedure

Preheat the oven to 400°F (200°C).

In a saucepan, place the sliced onion and the cocoa powder. Stir in the water, bring just to a boil, then cover the saucepan and cook over very low heat for 40 minutes. When done, blend to a smooth puree and reserve.

In a *sauteuse* or roasting pan, heat the butter and oil until almost smoking, then add the duck and brown on all sides. When nicely browned, place the duck on its back, arrange the wing tips, neck, and vegetables all around it, and place in the oven to roast for 20 minutes.

Remove the duck from the oven. Cut off the legs, put them back in the roasting pan, and continue roasting them for 10 more minutes. Separate the breasts and keep them warm on a plate underneath an overturned bowl while the legs finish cooking. When the legs are done, add them to the plate with the breasts, cover once more, and keep warm in the oven with the door ajar (lower the oven to 300°F [150°C]).

Pour off all the fat in the roasting pan, then add the Grand Marnier to the vegetables, neck, and wings, scraping the bottom of the pan to detach any caramelized juices stuck to it; add the orange juice, still scraping, then allow to cook at a moderate boil until all the liquid has evaporated. Add the stock, melted chocolate, and 4 generous teaspoons of the cocoa-onion mixture and boil gently for 10 minutes.

While the sauce finishes cooking, cut the breastmeat into thin slices. Arrange them in a circle or fan in the center of hot dinner plates, place a leg in the middle of each one, and spoon the sauce all around. Serve immediately, garnished with orange sections, candied orange peel, and apple wedges lightly caramelized by being sautéed in a mixture of butter and sugar until golden brown and tender.

INGREDIENTS FOR 2 SERVINGS

1 onion, thinly sliced

2 teaspoons unsweetened cocoa powder

6½ tablespoons (100 ml) water

2 tablespoons (30 g) butter

3 tablespoons (50 ml) oil

One 2¼- to 2¾-pound (1 to 1¼ kg) duck, ready for roasting (keep the neck and wing tips for making the sauce)

2 carrots, diced

1 onion, diced

2 tablespoons (30 ml) Grand Marnier liqueur

1⅓ cups (300 ml) freshly squeezed orange juice

2 cups (½ l) chicken stock

½ ounce (15 g) semisweet chocolate, melted

The Garnish

Orange sections, removed from membranes (see p. 71)

Candied orange peel, cut into julienne strips

Apple wedges, caramelized in butter and sugar

PREPARATION TIME

The duck—50 to 55 minutes; the sauce—1 hour

Partridges Navarra Style

PERDRIX À LA MODE DE NAVARRE

INGREDIENTS FOR 4 SERVINGS

4 partridges, trussed as for roasting
Salt
3 tablespoons (50 ml) cooking oil
6 tablespoons (100 g) lard
2 cloves garlic, peeled
Pepper
2 cloves
1 cup (¼ l) dry white or red wine
½ cup (120 ml) wine vinegar
1 cup (¼ l) chicken stock or water
1 bay leaf
16 to 20 baby onions, peeled
1 ounce (30 g) semisweet chocolate, grated

PREPARATION TIME

1½ to 1¾ hours

This is an old Spanish recipe found in a Spanish magazine dating from the turn of the century. Like many dishes of that time, it's one that cooks very slowly, for a relatively long time.

Procedure

Salt the partridges inside and out.

In a frying pan, place half the oil and lard and heat until very hot. Add the partridges and brown on all sides over moderate heat, then lift them out of the fat and place them in a pot just large enough to hold them comfortably; reserve.

In the same fat and frying pan the partridges browned in, brown the garlic cloves over moderate heat, then add them and the fat to the partridges. Season with salt, pepper, and the cloves. Add the wine, vinegar, stock or water, and bay leaf. Bring to a boil, then lower the heat, cover the pot, and allow to simmer slowly for 40 minutes.

While the partridges are cooking, brown the baby onions in the rest of the oil and lard; reserve on a plate.

When the 40 minutes cooking time is up, add the grated chocolate to the pot, stirring it into the sauce, then add the baby onions. Continue cooking, covered, for 20 minutes more or until the onions are soft and the partridges perfectly tender. With a skimmer or slotted spoon, lift the partridges out of the sauce and place them on a hot serving platter deep enough to hold the sauce (if you like, you may cut the partridges in half).

Lift the bay leaf, cloves, and garlic cloves out of the sauce and taste for seasoning, adding salt and pepper if necessary. Pour the sauce and onions over the partridges and serve immediately.

Chicken and Lobster Catalan Style

LANGOUSTE ET POULET À LA CATALANE

This is an old Spanish recipe in which the flavors of the chicken and shellfish blend slowly with those of the seasonings and chocolate.

Procedure

Tie the bay leaf, thyme, parsley, leeks, and dried orange peel together in a bunch with kitchen string.

Peel the tomatoes by dropping them into a pot of boiling water and leaving them there for 20 to 30 seconds; drain, cool under running water, and peel. Cut them in half crosswise and press gently to squeeze out the seeds and liquid. Dice and reserve.

Brown the almonds as described on page 118 and reserve.

Mix the salt, pepper, and cinnamon together and rub the pieces of chicken with the mixture.

In a pot, heat the butter and ¼ cup of the oil over moderate heat and brown the pieces of chicken on all sides. When golden brown, add the onions. As soon as the onions begin to brown, sprinkle in the flour and stir to cook the flour for about 1 minute. Add the Banyuls and brandy or vodka, boil for 30 seconds, then add the tomatoes and stock (the pieces of chicken should be barely covered). Cover the pot and simmer for 30 minutes.

Meanwhile, place the almonds, garlic, saffron, and the chicken liver in a heavy-duty blender or food processor and blend to a paste. Stir in the grated chocolate.

A few minutes before the 30 minutes' cooking time is up, kill the lobster by plunging the tip of a large knife into the slit where the head meets the tail. Chop the lobster into 8 pieces with a cleaver (see note). Heat 2 tablespoons of the oil in a frying pan until almost smoking, and sauté the pieces of lobster over very high heat until no longer transparent.

When the chicken is finished cooking, stir the chocolate-almond paste into the chicken's cooking liquid and add the pieces of lobster. Cover and cook for 30 minutes more.

Make croutons by frying the slices of French bread in oil in a frying pan; drain on paper towels.

When the chicken and lobster are done, lift them out of the pot and place on a hot serving platter deep enough to hold the sauce. Remove the bouquet of herbs from the pot and discard. Taste the sauce and add salt and pepper if necessary, then pour over the chicken and lobster. Arrange the croutons around the edge and serve.

Note: The spiny or Florida lobster is a clawless lobster of warm waters; only the tail is eaten. If using a Maine lobster, cut the tail into 4 pieces, the claws into 2 pieces each. In either case, discard the head. Ed.

INGREDIENTS FOR 4 SERVINGS

1 bay leaf
1 sprig thyme
2 sprigs parsley
2 small leeks
1-inch-long (2.5 cm) piece dried orange peel
4 medium tomatoes
¾ cup (60 g) slivered almonds
1 teaspoon salt
½ teaspoon pepper
¼ teaspoon ground cinnamon
One 2¼-pound (1 kg) chicken, cut into 8 pieces (plus the liver)
5 tablespoons (80 g) butter
Cooking oil
2 medium or 1 large onion, chopped
1 tablespoon (10 g) flour
½ cup (120 ml) Banyuls (a sweet wine from Roussillon) or port
2 tablespoons white fruit brandy or vodka
1 cup (¼ l) chicken stock or water
1 clove garlic
1 pinch saffron
1 ounce (30 g) semisweet chocolate, grated
One 2¼-pound (1 kg) live spiny (Florida) lobster (if unavailable, use a live Maine lobster) (see note)
8 slices French bread

PREPARATION TIME

1½ to 1¾ hours

Baked Chicken Mole Style

POULET À L'ÉTOUFFÉE EN MEXICAN MOLE

INGREDIENTS FOR 4 TO 5 SERVINGS

*One 28-ounce (850 ml) can
    peeled, whole tomatoes*
*2 tablespoons (25 g) granulated
    sugar*
2 tablespoons (20 g) flour
1 teaspoon chili powder
½ teaspoon ground cinnamon
*1½ ounces (40 g) semisweet
    chocolate*
½ cup (120 ml) chicken stock
1 medium onion, finely chopped
1 clove garlic, finely chopped
2 tablespoons cooking oil
*One 3-pound (1.4 kg) chicken,
    cut into 8 pieces*
Salt and pepper

PREPARATION TIME

1¾ to 2 hours

Procedure

Drain the tomatoes and chop them coarsely.

In a bowl, mix the sugar, flour, chili powder, and cinnamon; reserve.

In a small double boiler, melt the chocolate; little by little, stir in the chicken stock; reserve.

Preheat the oven to 400°F (200°C).

In a *sauteuse* or high-sided frying pan, brown the onion and garlic in the oil over moderate heat. Add the flour-spice mixture, stirring, and continue cooking until the flour begins to brown very lightly. Stir in the tomatoes, chocolate-flavored stock, salt, and pepper. Bring to a boil, then lower the heat and simmer, stirring occasionally, for 5 to 10 minutes.

Arrange the pieces of chicken in a low-sided casserole or roasting pan. Pour over the sauce, then cover with a sheet of aluminum foil and the cover of the casserole, or tape the foil in place in order to tightly seal the roasting pan. Place in the oven and bake for 1 hour. At the end of the cooking time, check to see if the chicken is perfectly tender; if not, cover and cook a little longer. Serve in the casserole or roasting pan, accompanied with plain rice.

Index

About the Author

Well-known in gourmet circles both here and abroad, Martine Jolly is one of France's most talented cookbook authors. She is married to Claude Jolly, a cookbook publisher and food critic. They live in Paris.